THE ILLUSTRATED HISTORY OF Albion VEHICLES

MUSSELBURGH TOWN COUNCIL
ROADS DEPT.
4

THE ILLUSTRATED HISTORY OF

Albion

VEHICLES

NICK BALDWIN

A **FOULIS** Motoring Book

Fisrt published 1988

Published by:
Haynes Publishing Group
Sparkford, Nr. Yeovil, Somerset
BA22 7JJ. England

Haynes Publications Inc.
861 Lawrence Drive, Newbury Park,
California 91320 USA

British Library Cataloging in Publication Data

Baldwin, Nick
The illustrated history of Albion vehicles.
1. Albion commercial vehicles, to 1987
I. Title
629.2'24

ISBN 0-85429-686-7

Library of Congress catalog card number 88-81069

Editor: Robert Iles
Page Layout: Phil Lyons
Printed in England by:
J.H. Haynes & Co. Ltd.

ALBION
N-5636

Acknowledgements

My thanks to everyone who has made this book possible, including my late colleagues, Prince Marshall, the proprietor of *Old Motor Magazine* who collected so many commercial vehicle archives, and Michael Sedgwick, the doyen of motoring historians who helped to make serious interest in such vehicles a "respectable" pastime. His work lives on with the Michael Sedgwick Memorial Trust, which is always anxious to receive funds as well as manuscripts and research that explore the lesser known facets of motoring history. More details of the Trust can be obtained from the Hon. Secretary, G.B. Heath, Spring Cottage, 20 High Street, Milford on Sea, Lymington, Hampshire. The photographs in this book have come from too many sources to be named individually, but my thanks to all concerned. Thanks also to Haynes/Foulis for continuing to be one of the very few publishers to take an interest in commercial vehicle history. So far they have produced Leyland, Dennis and now Ford and Albion in this series, as well as a look at the history of off-road vehicles. In the near future they intend to continue to take a pictorial look at some of the other great names of British road transport – names like Seddon-Atkinson, ERF, Foden, Thornycroft, Guy, Scammell and Commer/Karrier.

Introduction

Albion made commercial vehicles for over seventy years and for most of that period was by far Scotland's most important producer. Its vehicles had an air of rugged, no frills independence about them. They made little attempt at modernity or fashionable styling and were as fiercely proud of their grecian-style radiator as any Rolls-Royce. They soldiered on bravely with four cylinders long after most of their rivals had moved to six. The sunburst motif was one of the best known trademarks in the industry and the claim "as sure as the sunrise" was absolutely undoubted by operators the world over.

Though no vehicles have been made since 1972 under the Albion name the Glasgow factories have continued to flourish and Albion hub reduction axles have become a byword for reliability. Many of the famous old model names continued on Leylands into the 1980s and thousands of Albions and Albion derived vehicles are still in use. Fortunately many more of the earlier examples have been preserved for posterity and examples are to be found at the National Motor Museum Beaulieu, the transport museum at Glasgow and the British Commercial Vehicle Museum at Leyland as well as in the hands of numerous private enthusiasts.

Though Scotland was once one of the great industrial centres of Europe its traditional heavy industries have contracted and in retrospect one can see that Albion picked the wrong place to be born. Sentinel realised this when it moved from Glasgow to Shrewsbury soon after the Great War and Beardmore's vehicle side was later to follow suit and go to its main market of London. Albion's early successes in London actually played right into the hands of its agents in the capital, who soon made their own Lacre vehicles to compete with Albion.

Apart from the English firms, the principal rival to Albion in the first half of its life was Halley, and it was perhaps appropriate that, when this firm finally succumbed to the might of the Great Depression and Albion's strength, its factory should be taken over by its vanquisher. Albion was canny in paying nothing for Halley's goodwill and having nothing further to do with the marque and yet pinching some of its wonderful Scottish model names!

An idea of Albion's importance can be gauged by its becoming the first of Leyland's takeovers. This took place nearly forty years ago and soon after AEC had started its own empire building by acquiring Maudslay and Crossley. Henceforth it was to be a battle between AEC and Leyland and ultimately the world's major truck producers.

Albion was not interfered with too drastically during this period and undoubtedly it benefited from its Leyland connections. It became the light- and mid-weight specialist and ultimately built up to being the major British producer of six-wheelers in the 1960s and 70s. The success of these was due to competitive pricing, Leyland engines and the famous "unbreakable" Albion axles, which continue to be its forte. One can only hope that despite the Leyland DAF merger of 1987 this speciality will continue long into the future.

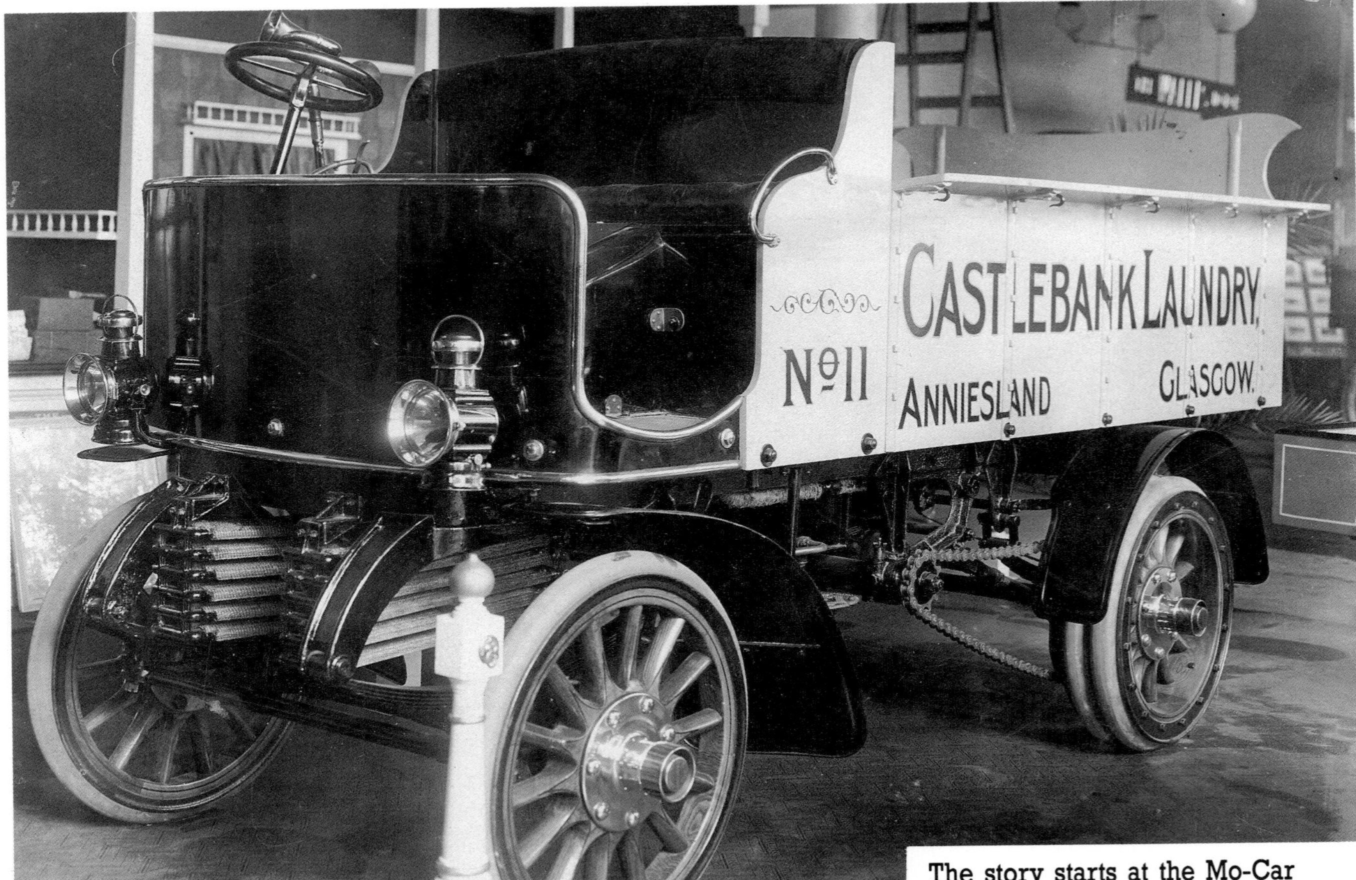

The story starts at the Mo-Car Syndicate, formed in 1895 with financial backing from Sir William Arrol, consulting engineer and designer of the Forth Bridge. George Johnston, who had worked for the Hydepark Locomotive Co., developed a petrol engined dogcart in 1895 and this entered series production in 1896/7 as the Arrol Johnston. One of the company's early commercial vehicles is shown here, which despite its archaic looks, actually postdates the first Albion by a few years.

Norman O. Fulton was works manager at Arrol Johnston and T. Blackwood Murray was commercial manager. The latter had earlier developed a low tension magneto whilst working for engineers Mavor and Coulson and in 1899 he and Fulton left to start the Albion Motor Car Company. Their factory consisted of 3,600 square feet of upstairs space above the Clan Line repair shops in Finnieston Street, Glasgow, where they employed seven men and had two lathes and two drill presses.

Their first dogcart took to the road in 1900 and employed an opposed twin 8 hp engine similar to the Arrol Johnston but with T. Blackwood Murray's patent magneto and governor. The 159th Albion dogcart was sold during 1903 and here we see an early example outside Perth Post Office in 1901. The two gentlemen in the 1900 A2 are the founders N.O. Fulton (driving) and T. Blackwood Murray.

The first Albion to be exported was this 8 hp chassis for Kuala Lumpur. The date was claimed to be 1901, though 1902 seems more likely as this was when wheel, as opposed to tiller, steering was standardised. This photo was probably taken in later life so maybe the vehicle's steering had been modified by then.

The original A2 was also available as an 8 hp half-ton van and this is the first one to be produced in 1902, the year in which Albion became a private limited company. Albion won a silver medal in the Automobile Club of Great Britain and Ireland Five Hundred Mile Trial with an A2, and won numerous other reliability awards between 1901 and 1908. The Scotstoun works referred to here was two hundred yards from the Clyde and in full production from the summer of 1903. It initially had a floor area of 41,680 square feet. Part of the old Finnieston Street works became the home of the Bergius marine engine firm which also made a few cars, whilst another part housed the Glasgow Motor Lorry Co., which became Halley's Industrial Vehicles Ltd.

The A3 model had a twin vertical cylinder 12 (later 16) horsepower engine and first appeared in 1903. It replaced the dogcarts and was joined by increasingly heavy goods versions from 1904. In 1906 a four-cylinder 24 hp version was offered and production that year totalled 221 chassis from a workforce of 283. By 1910 the factory had grown to 120,000 square feet and 450 men and it was in this era that the chain driven tanker shown here was built. The imposing building is the office headquarters of the Albion Motor Car Co.

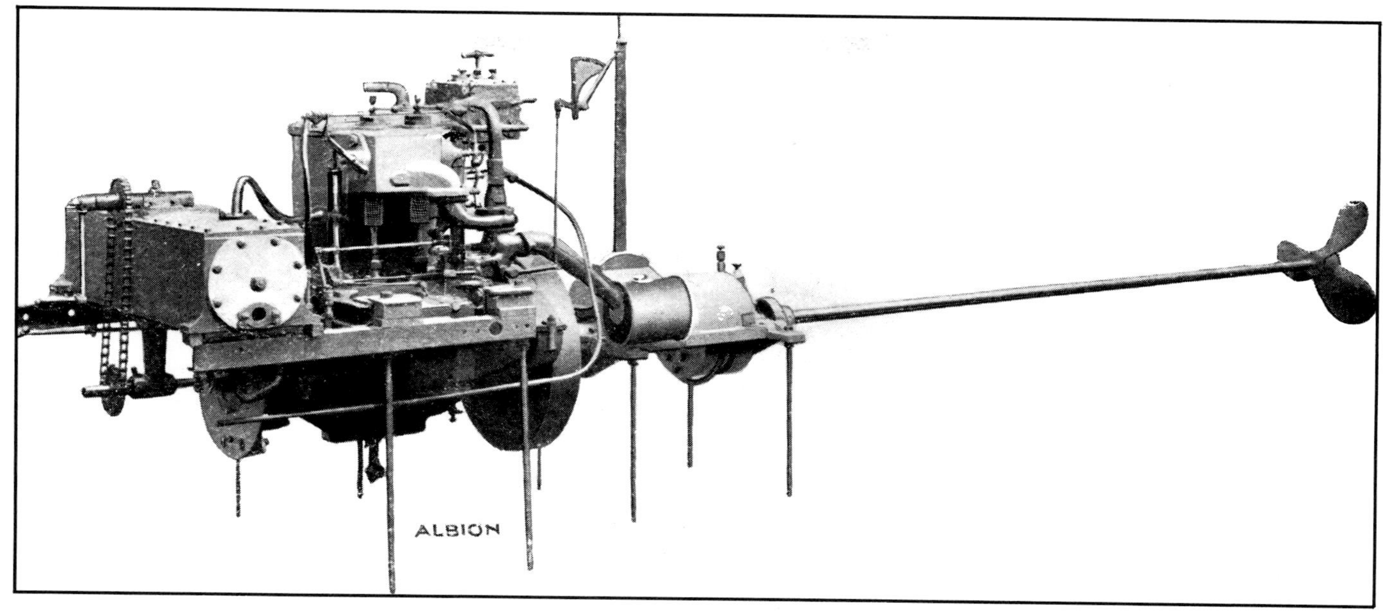

As well as complete vehicles Albion also offered engines for various purposes. Shown here is their 15 hp marine set complete at £192 (they also made 12 and 24 hp petrol and paraffin versions) and a Barford and Perkins roller available in five- to eight-ton sizes with 16 hp Albion engines.

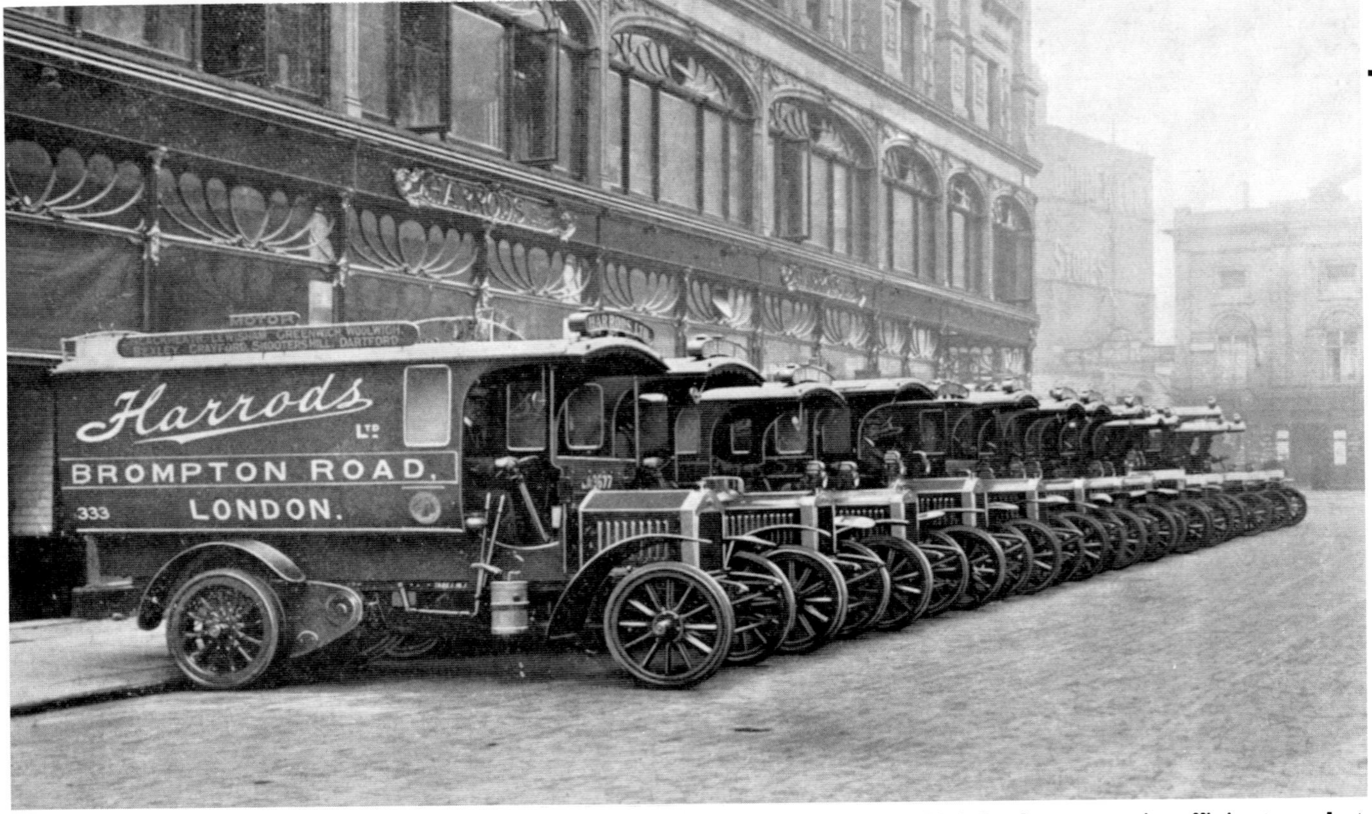

Plainly there was insufficient market for Albion vehicles in Scotland alone and the Long Acre Motor Car Company helped to establish the marque in London. There, many of the big stores bought Albions with Lacre bodywork. By the 'teens Harrods had acquired no less than seventy Albions and this figure soon grew to 103. There were also many other big fleets. From 1909 not all these sales went to Albion as by then the Lacre Motor Car Co. Ltd., as it was known, had become a maker of complete vehicles in its own right.

Albion claimed to be the largest manufacturer of motor vans in the British Empire in the 'teens. Here is a small selection used in the laundry trade. Albion's catalogues were full of testimonials to the fine service given by the vehicles. J.S. Fry spoke of 10,000 miles in a year with no hitch or breakdown. Inglis Bakery of Belfast had covered 30,000 miles without a hiccup and Federal Stores in Kuala Lumpur did 80 to 120 miles per day, whilst Ottawa Valley Motor Transit had four Albions which covered 488 aggregate miles in a day delivering mail. Albion predicted that their vehicles would survive 150,000 to 200,000 miles or a minimum of ten years.

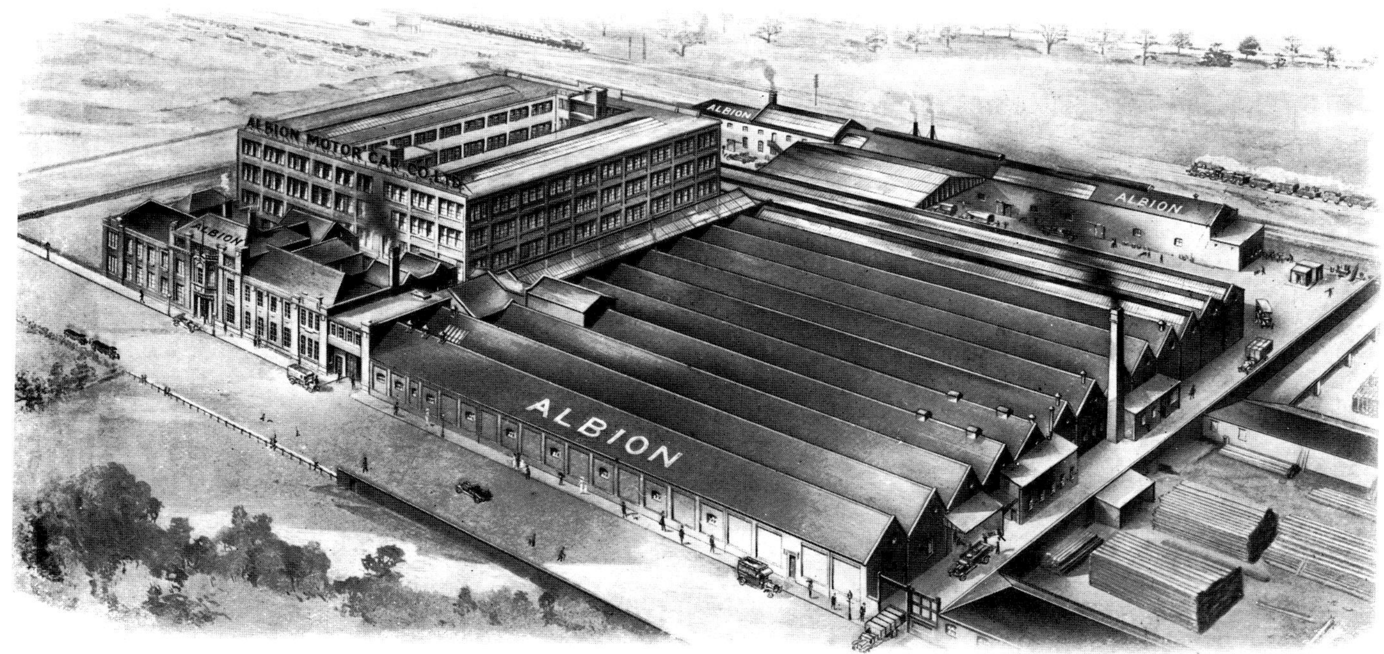

An artist's impression of the Scotstoun Works shortly before the Great War. By then the firm had four Managing Directors consisting of the two founders plus John Henderson and Norman Fulton's brother Ernest.

An Albion one-tonner had won a gold medal in the prestigious RAC Industrial Vehicle Trials and this had helped to make the Scottish firm even better known outside its homeland. Here is a ton van lavishly bodied in London by Hora for a well-known maker of cigarettes. Such was the success of Albion and its compatriots that in 1909 the journal *Commercial Motor* was moved to comment: "The English Invasion of Scotland can never equal the reverse order of events – too many Scottish vehicles continue to be steadily poured over the border each month".

In 1910 Albion introduced the 3 to 4 ton A10 32 hp model, which was to become their staple product. It had a monobloc four-cylinder engine incorporating Blackwood Murray patent governor and lubricator, a separate gearbox and chain drive.

Right: An assortment of Albion psvs and their users. The vehicles shown are all based on the A10 chassis and appear in a sales brochure dating from about 1912. In 1913 Albion introduced a 25 seat torpedo charabanc at the Scottish Motor Show that had doors, a roof and remarkably advanced streamlined styling.

Albions in the Public Service

32 h.p. Albion Char-a-banc. Supplied to Kingswinford and Wolverhampton Motor Bus Service, Kingswinford, Staffs.

ENGLAND

STANDFIELD & WHITE, Ltd. ... ... Exeter
WOLVERHAMPTON CORPORATION TRAMWAY CO., Ltd., Wolverhampton
KINGSWINFORD & WOLVERHAMPTON MOTOR BUS SERVICE ... ... Staffs
ROBERTS BROS. ... ... Holyhead
R. RITCHIE ... ... Maryport
J. BLAKE & CO. ... ... Manchester and Liverpool
ANNFIELD PLAIN & DISTRICT MOTOR CO.... Durham
ROBT. BOAD & SONS ... ... So. Hetton
COLDINGHAM MOTOR BUS CO. ... ...Coldingham

32 h.p. 30 seater Char-a-banc. Supplied to H.M. The Amir of Afghanistan.

SCOTLAND & IRELAND

GLEN URQUHART MOTOR CAR CO., Ltd., Drumnadrochit
FORFAR MOTOR VEHICLE CO. ... ... Forfar
OBAN, FORD & LOCH AWE SYNDICATE, Ltd. Loch Awe
WEST KILBRIDE MOTOR & HIRING CO., Ltd., West Kilbride
D. MacBRAYNE, Ltd. ... ... Fort William
LARGS, WEMYSS BAY & WEST COAST MOTOR SERVICE ... ... Largs
CAITHNESS & SUTHERLAND MOTOR CO., Ltd., Thurso
SUTHERLAND MOTOR TRAFFIC CO. ... ... Lairg
BELFAST & PORT-A-FERRY PASSENGER & MAIL SERVICE ... ... Belfast

FOREIGN

SYDNEY TRAMWAYS ... ... N.S.W.
NAAS-WELLBROOK MOTOR TRANSPORT CO., N.S.W.
COBB & CO.... ... ... Perth, W.A.
MORNINGTON BOROUGH COUNCIL ... New Zealand
CRAIG & CO. ... ... Dunedin, N.Z.
JOHANNESBURG TRAMWAYS ... ... South Africa
SOUTH INDIA COMMERCIAL CORPORATION, Ltd., Madura, India
MYSORE COORG MOTOR TRANSPORT CO., Ltd., India
BURMA MOTOR TRANSPORT CO. ... ... Burma
BUCKINGHAM RAPID TRANSPORT CO., Ltd. Canada
GREATER OTTAWA DEVELOPMENT CO. ... Canada
STRAITS & F.M.S. MOTOR SERVICE CO., Ltd., Penang
ESTEBAN NOCETTI ... ... Argentine
HOSEIN BAKSH ... ... Trinidad

32 h.p. 29 seater Char-a-banc, purchased by Annfield Plain & District Motor Co., Durham.

32 h.p. 30 seater Albion Char-a-banc. Supplied to Largs, Wemyss Bay and West Coast Motor Service, Largs, Scotland.

GOVERNMENTS

H.M. WAR OFFICE
H.M. INDIA OFFICE
AUSTRALIAN GOVERNMENT
NEW ZEALAND GOVERNMENT
TASMANIAN GOVERNMENT
SOUTH AFRICAN GOVERNMENT
SOUTHERN NIGERIA GOVERNMENT
NEGRI SEMBILAN GOVERNMENT
NYASSALAND GOVERNMENT
UGANDA GOVERNMENT
SIERRA LEONE GOVERNMENT
GOLD COAST GOVERNMENT
CEYLON GOVERNMENT
H.M. THE AMIR OF AFGHANISTAN
STRAITS SETTLEMENTS GOVERNMENT
DUTCH EAST INDIES GOVERNMENT

A very spartan looking A10 supplied to A. and T. Hovell of Carnoustie. When not used as a lorry it received a slightly more luxurious charabanc body, both types having been built by the Westfield Autocar Co. of Gorgie, Edinburgh.

In 1912 about 150 of the 554 Albions made were cars and the directors decided that henceforth the thousand men at Scotstoun would concentrate on commercial vehicles plus a few shooting brakes and estate cars based on van chassis. Here we see one of the last Albion pleasure cars, a laundaulette bodied by Wm. Millan and Sons of Falkirk. It is Albion's largest, a 24/30 hp four-cylinder, other types made being a two-cylinder 16 hp machine and, in the final year, a 15 hp four-cylinder shaft driven car. The 16 hp model carrying baskets and a dog belonged to J.R.B. Elliot of Harwood, Hawick.

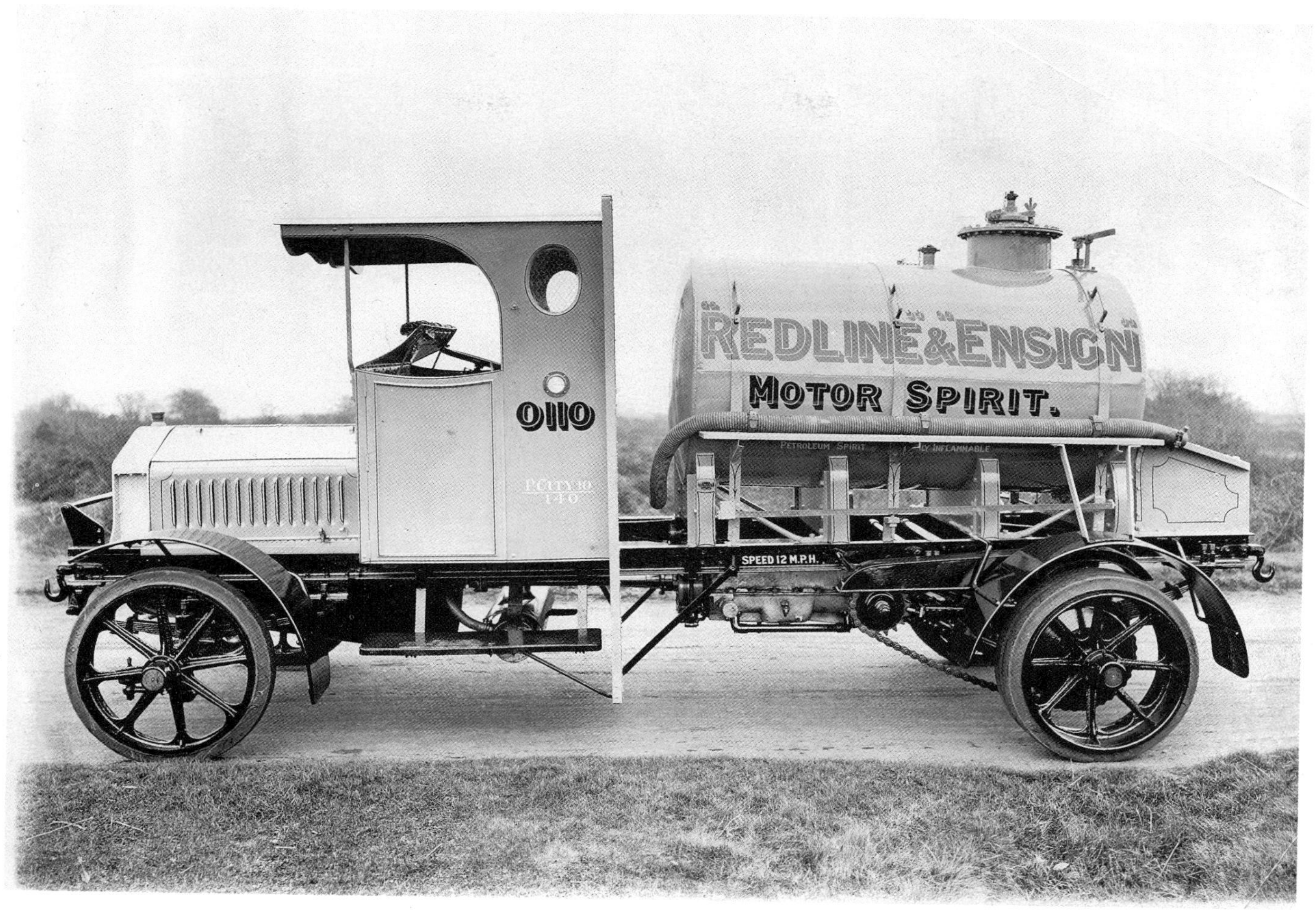

This A10 was fitted with tanker bodywork by Fry Brothers Ltd. of Greenwich. Note the fire shield and under-cab exhaust system required by the petroleum regulations. Also clearly visible is the position of the gearbox and cross-shaft for the chain final drive. A few shaft driven Albions were also built in the 'teens.

An assortment of Albions at work during the 1914/18 War. Approximately six thousand A10 lorries were supplied, making Albion one of the top half dozen producers in Britain. The factory expanded many times in the war years and for his contribution T. Blackwood Murray was made an honorary Doctor of Science by Edinburgh University in 1917. He had obtained a civil engineering degree at Edinburgh in 1890. The convoy of Albions shown here was incidentally used to ferry supplies over the Khyber Pass where the lorries started in sub-tropical heat and reached the icy peak after hours of arduous climbing.

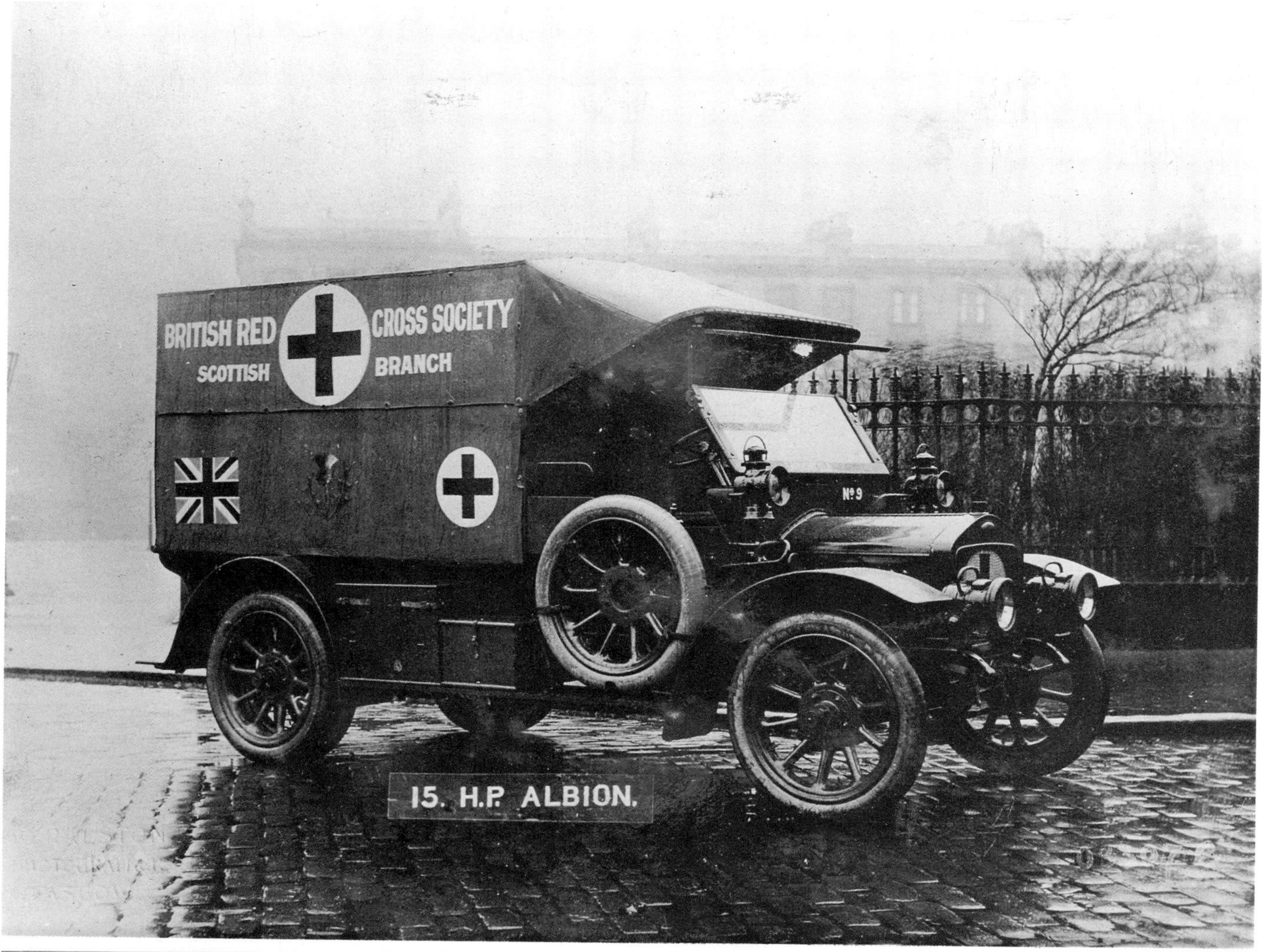

15. H.P ALBION.

The A10 was widely available in the 1920s both as an ex-WD vehicle and new from the factory. By the time that production ended in 1926 a total of nine thousand had been sold.

T. Blackwood Murray was quick to develop new models despite the postwar slump and his 20 horsepower $1^1/2$ ton capacity SB24 of 1922/3 was the first to qualify under the new Subsidy Scheme. Operators received £40 a year for three years in exchange for keeping their vehicles in readiness for military call up. If required they would be bought by the War Department under favourable terms. The following pictures of the SB24, including a big dairy fleet in Australia, give some idea of the wide number of roles played by the light Albions. Note that all have solid tyres except the station bus caught midway, with solids on the back wheels and pneumatics on the front, and the lorry on military trial in 1924 with off-road balloon tyres. The large Nestlés fleet was at work in Sydney, New South Wales.

McVitie & Price
BY SPECIAL APPOINTMENT
TO HIS MAJESTY
KING GEORGE. V.
DIGESTIVE BISCUITS
29
20 H.P. ALBION

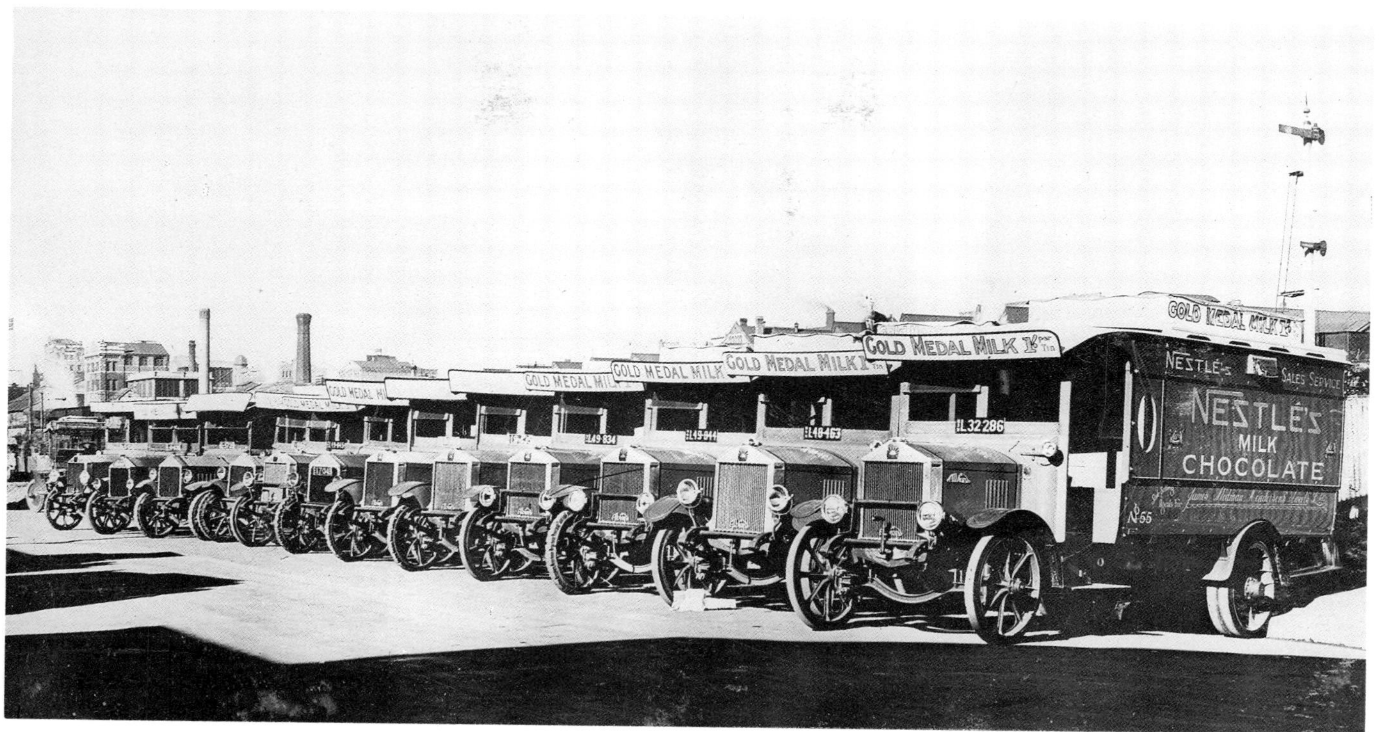

GOLD MEDAL MILK
GOLD MEDAL MILK
GOLD MEDAL MILK
GOLD MEDAL MILK
NESTLÉ'S SALES SERVICE
NESTLÉ'S
MILK
CHOCOLATE
L 32 286

Albion
161

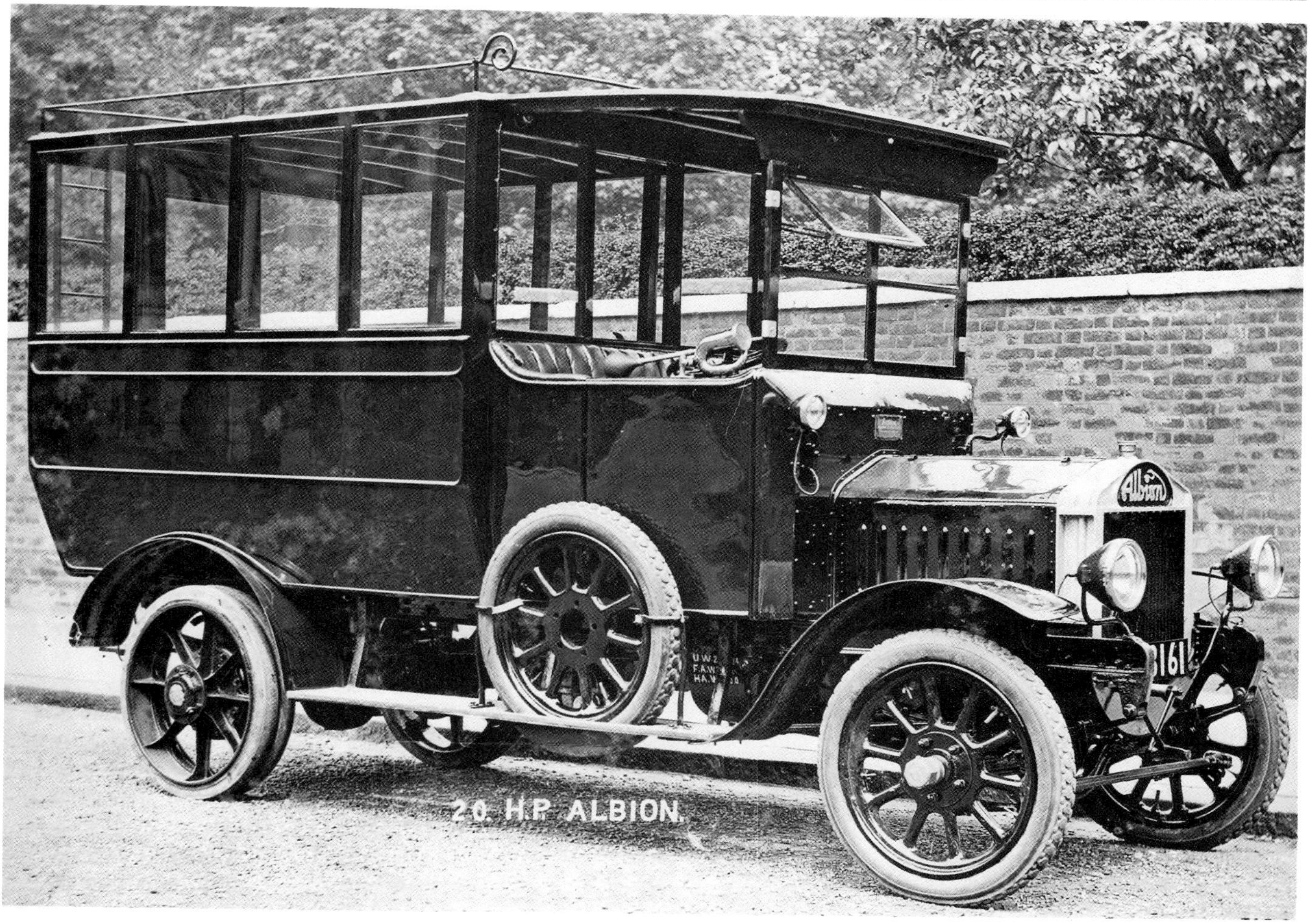

20. H.P. ALBION.

Albions had very long lives, the author discovering that virtually all the transport on the island of Bute, where he holidayed around 1960, comprised Albions of the 1920s and 1930s. Here is a circa 1920 lorry that was later relegated to rail shunting duties before being photographed in a scrapyard in the 1960s.

Two views of Albions in select company. The Bryant and May lorries are Thornycrofts with a Leyland in the distance and an Albion in the foreground, whilst in the warehouse view the Albions outnumber the Leyland three to one. The Brymay vehicles are in one of the concours parades that encouraged drivers to keep their charges spotless. Note the smart chauffeurs' uniforms.

Albion's first forward control model (a layout that Albion persistently called overtype) came at the end of 1924. It was known as the Mark III and was for 3 or 4 ton loads. The Mark II was a normal control chassis of similar capacity. An interesting feature of the Mark III was the way the front wings were attached to the doors to ease access to both the cab and the sides of the engine. A rather similar wing arrangement was soon patented by Garner, though in their case the doors were not attached to the wings.

The chassis of a 30 horsepower shaft driven Model 27 three-tonner in 1925 and a view of some in service with United Dairies and their associates, Mickleover Transport. These milk carriers had a fleet of 188 Albions at the time consisting of $1^1/_2$ ton, 2 ton, 3 and 4 ton types.

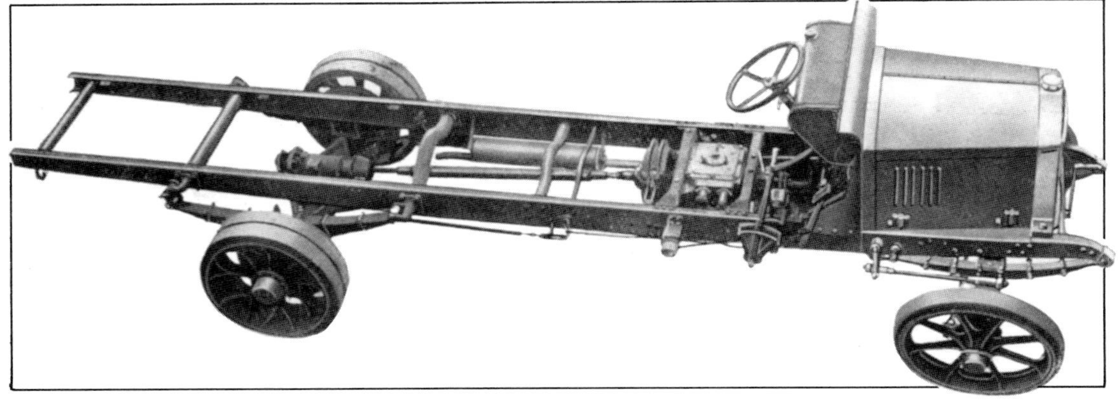

From 1923 Albion offered one of the first low-frame bus chassis to be available on the open market (the products of the pioneers, AEC, were by then freely available, but the vast majority went for LGOC use). Albion called their newcomer the Viking and gave it a most attractive radiator reminiscent of their old highgrade touring cars. Hicks Bros., of Felstead, Essex, ran this 30/60 hp charabanc and commented in 1925 "owing to the extremely comfortable springing, customers prefer it to any other vehicle. The running cost is quite satisfactory". Fourteen-and eighteen-seat versions were offered, with twenty seats from 1926.

As well as the low frame types, Albion offered a 30/60 hp four-cylinder model with semi-dropped frame from 1925. It came in 25 or 29 passenger guise or for 32 passengers with forward control. The chassis price ranged from £745 to £815 and in this instance the bodywork was by Phoenix of Farnham.

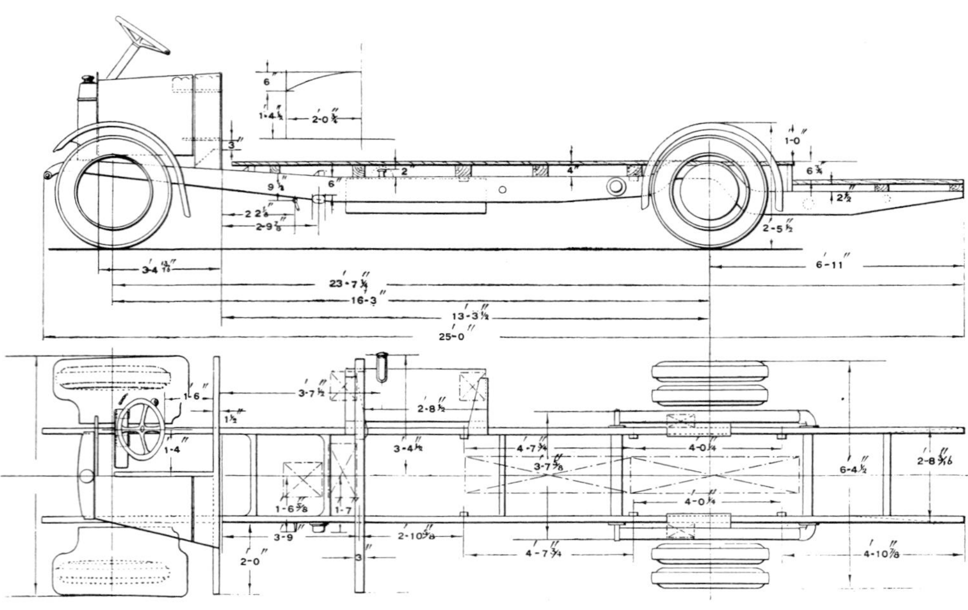

The forward control version of the 30/60 hp was widely used. Scottish Motor Traction ordered 24 in March 1927 which is the year in which this bodybuilder's layout drawing was prepared. Note the relatively low chassis line and the provision for a low step rear entrance. The advertisement depicting a Londonderry Corporation 30/60 dates from November 1928. In 1925 a 30/60 demonstrator completed the round trip from Glasgow to London and back to Glasgow in a little over twenty-four hours.

30/60 h.p. 32-Seater Rear Entrance Overtype 'Bus supplied to the Londonderry Corporation.

The original 30 cwt. Subsidy chassis evolved through the 1920s and continued as a two-tonner long after the Subsidy Scheme was forgotten. Here we have a small selection from the mid 1920s and onwards. The bus is bodied by Hall-Lewis of Park Royal and dates from 1925, the fire appliances belonged to Melbourne and Metropolitan Fire Brigade, the advertisement showing the ingeniously liveried Cooper's Teas van dates from 1928, as does the timber lorry which is very similar to the first vehicle preserved by the author in the 1960s. The Huntley and Palmer sample dispenser is an attractive outfit and the White Horse SB24 model dates from January 1926. The most modern is the Merrie England M43 of 1931. Note the gradual appearance of the "sure as sunrise" radiator.

HUNTLEY & PALMERS.
BISCUITS.
DP-5741
THIS IS
THE VAN
THE BOYS
WHO DELIVER
Huntley & Palmers
SAMPLE DELIVERY.
THE SAMPLES
ARE BISCUITS
AND GIVEN
QUITE FREE
DELIGHTFUL
FOR BREAKFAST
FOR DINNER
FOR TEA
SUPERIOR
HUNTLEY & PALMERS LTD
READING BISCUITS.
Albion

WHITE HORSE WHISKY.
WHITE HORSE DISTILLERS LTD.
The White Horse Cellar
Est. 1742
BY APPOINTMENT
WHITE HORSE
DISTILLERS
LIMITED
GLASGOW.

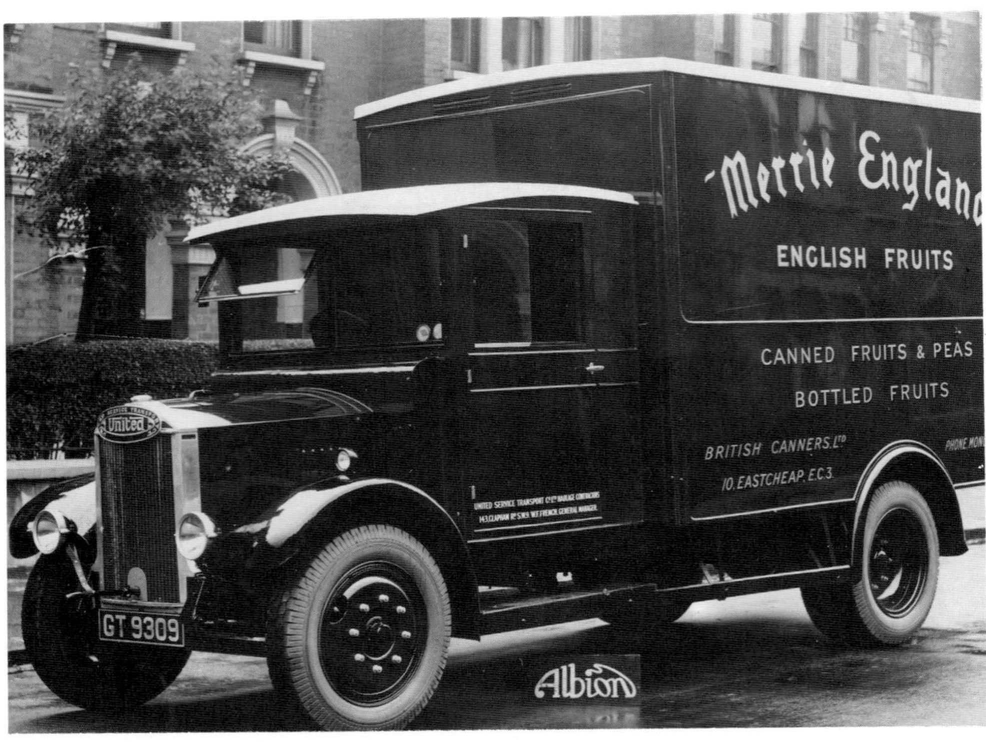

TYPICAL HALL - LEWIS COACHWORK FOR THE ALBION MOTOR CAR CO., LTD.

14-seater Station Bus or Shooting Brake, with detachable seats and large double doors at rear. Entrance from front, also. Built for the Albion Motor Car Co., Ltd., on their Model 24 chassis by

HALL, LEWIS & Co., Ltd.

SALES OFFICE: 14, Cockspur St., London, S.W.1 ('Phone: Gerrard 8933). Works: Park Royal.

TEST FOR YOURSELF THE OUTSTANDING MERITS

OF THE NEW 30 cwt ALBION

CHASSIS PRICE
(*Ex-Works, Glasgow.*)

£365

Complete with 33"×5" pneumatics front, 34"×7" pneumatics rear, spare wheel with solid tyre and carrier, 12 volt. 5 lamp lighting set and electric horn, speedometer and front wings.

LET us send you the new 20/36 h.p. Albion 30-cwt. chassis to examine and try out in comparison with any other 30-cwt. vehicle on the market.

You will be astonished by the proof you can obtain of its outstanding mechanical efficiency, its exceptionally powerful braking, its lightness and speed (attaining over 40 m.p.h.) and the sturdy construction which ensures absolute dependability for an unusual length of life.

And you can prove for yourself that **it is definitely superior to any other 30-cwt. vehicle on the market.** Write for full details of this new Albion.

TAXATION
The unladen weight of standard complete vehicles is under 2 tons.

30-cwt. Albion Box Van supplied to Messrs. Cooper & Co.'s Stores, Limited.

Albion
COMMERCIAL MOTORS
ALBION MOTOR CAR CO., LTD.
SCOTSTOUN GLASGOW.
London: BANK BUILDINGS, 20 KINGSWAY, W.C.2
Also at MANCHESTER,
LEEDS, SHEFFIELD, BIRMINGHAM AND BRISTOL

Most Albion vehicles had a traditional look that lasted well into the 1950s. Despite this the firm was surprisingly avant garde and, as we have seen, was early to make six-cylinder passenger types and drop frame chassis. Its vehicles were generally lighter than competitive vehicles, despite Forth Bridge-like engineering. In 1927 a very advanced looking 35/55 hp forward control range appeared with faired-in radiator shell. The four-tonner, followed by a five-tonner in 1928, had a worm driven rear axle and a cab that could be lifted off by crane for major engine maintenance. The five-tonner had Clayton Dewandre servo brakes. The advertisements date from 1928 (solid tyres) and 1930, whilst the photographs include a Shell tanker of 1930, a Lyons flat bed of 1928, a similar vehicle of 1927 belonging to Washington Chemical Co., and a 1930 gulley emptier carrying equipment by the famous steam engineers, Fowler of Leeds.

IN crowded docks, loading bays and other congested places where loading and turning are so difficult, the Albion 35/55 h.p. Overtype 4 and 5-tonners are invaluable.

These remarkable Albion models turn in a 48 ft. circle, and are therefore as "handy" as the average 2-tonner. They can carry a body 14 ft. 9 ins. long, with an overall length of only 21 feet.

The engine is readily accessible, and particularly powerful brakes are fitted. The brakes on the 5-tonner are operated through Servo Vacuum gear. Either pneumatic or solid tyres are provided.

Both models fully uphold the Albion's reputation for saving big sums in running and upkeep costs.

Write for particulars of these and other Albion models of 30-cwt. to 3-ton load capacity.

Albion
COMMERCIAL MOTORS
ALBION MOTOR CAR Co., LTD.
SCOTSTOUN, GLASGOW
London: - - BANK BUILDINGS, 20 KINGSWAY, W.C.2
Also at MANCHESTER, LEEDS, SHEFFIELD, BIRMINGHAM AND BRISTOL.

35/55 *h.p. 5-ton Albion Overtype Lorry delivered to Messrs. Harland & Wolff, Ltd.*

"WHY WE BOUGHT MORE ALBIONS" No 1

Messrs. COOPER & CO's STORES LTD

"RESULTS PROVED THEM ECONOMICAL AND RELIABLE"

HERE is what Messrs. Cooper & Co.'s Stores, Ltd., the well-known Grocers and Provision Merchants of Glasgow, Liverpool and London, say in a recent letter:—

"*During the past quarter of a century we have had working experience of practically all Albion goods models. Our first Albion was a 2-cylinder 2-tonner which covered nearly 200,000 miles on delivery work before being superseded by an up-to-date machine. We have continued to add more Albions to our fleet because the results obtained have proved them to be both economical and thoroughly reliable. Even on the arduous work entailed by our delivery service which extends throughout the Western Highlands, where bad roads abound, their performance has been in every way satisfactory.*"

[Messrs. Cooper's have purchased to date 49 Albions.]

Experiences such as this show clearly that it would be worth your while to consider using Albions. Let us send you a chassis for inspection. Load capacity 30-cwt. to 5-tons.

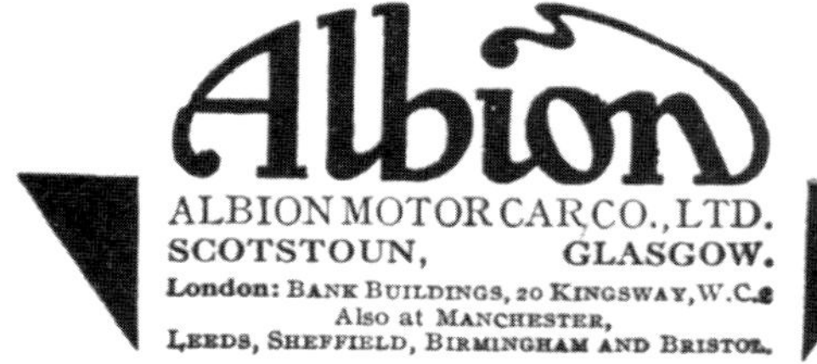

ALBION MOTOR CAR CO., LTD.
SCOTSTOUN, GLASGOW.
London: BANK BUILDINGS, 20 KINGSWAY, W.C.2
Also at MANCHESTER,
LEEDS, SHEFFIELD, BIRMINGHAM AND BRISTOL.

WRITE TO-DAY FOR FULL PARTICULARS

There can have been very few Albions in the AEC stronghold of the London General Omnibus Co. This example dates from 1929 and is believed to have joined the General via Land Development and Lewis. Nearly sixty Albions were used by the LPTB but these were virtually all lorries, ranging from welders to ticket offices and from catering vans to breakdown vehicles.

One of the strongest Albion enclaves south of the border was in Gloucestershire and South Wales, thanks to agent Arthur Watts. The Watts family were also involved with Red and White Motor Services, which ran this impressive long distance 30/60 hp coach. In 1929 Watts began experiments with a 30/60 engine converted to run on the compression ignition system and Albion took up the development, though it was not until 1933 that an Albion diesel was to be offered. This PR28 chassis has a 26-seat Strachans aluminium panelled body.

Albion had one great advantage not enjoyed by its southern competitors, and that was one vast hilly test track stretching hundreds of miles to the north of Glasgow. All the 20,942 vehicles built from the firm's beginning to the end of 1929 received a road test before sale and the factory also had a cross-country test course at Scotstoun for colonial and military chassis. 1929 was the year in whch co-founder Dr. T. Blackwood Murray died after a long illness. He had been living latterly at Montana in Switzerland. His partner, F. O. Fulton, died suddenly in 1935 and in his £141,390 will left £1,000 to Albion employee benevolent funds. George Pate held the post of Managing Director from 1933 to 1946 and was succeeded by Fulton's son, who had been with Albion since studying American techniques in 1928.

The Viking was also available with forward control and this is the Factory demonstrator of the late 1920s. The normal control version of the 36/90 hp was for 26 seats whilst the forward control type seated 32 and cost £50 more at £1,100 for the chassis.

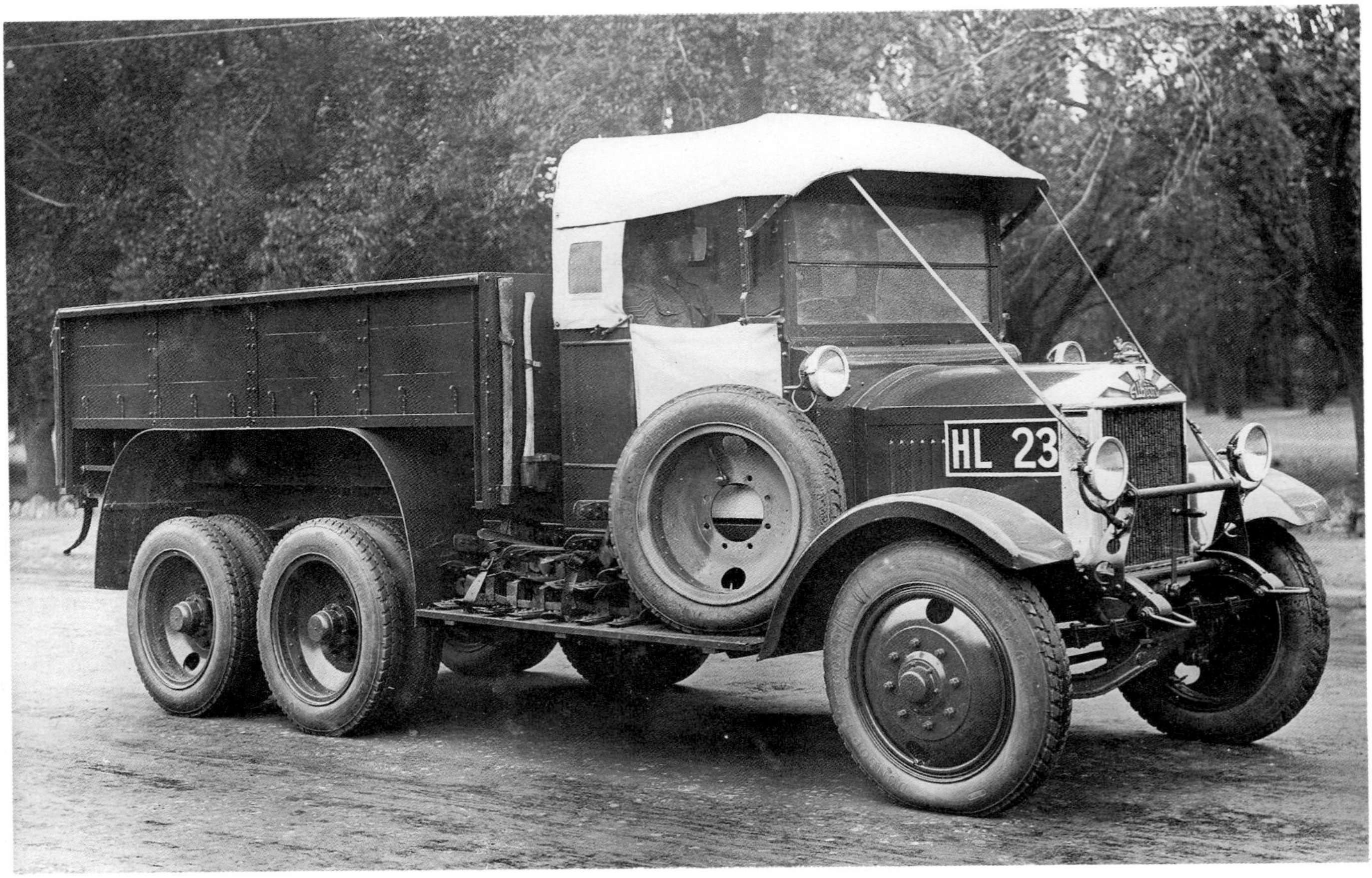
HL 23

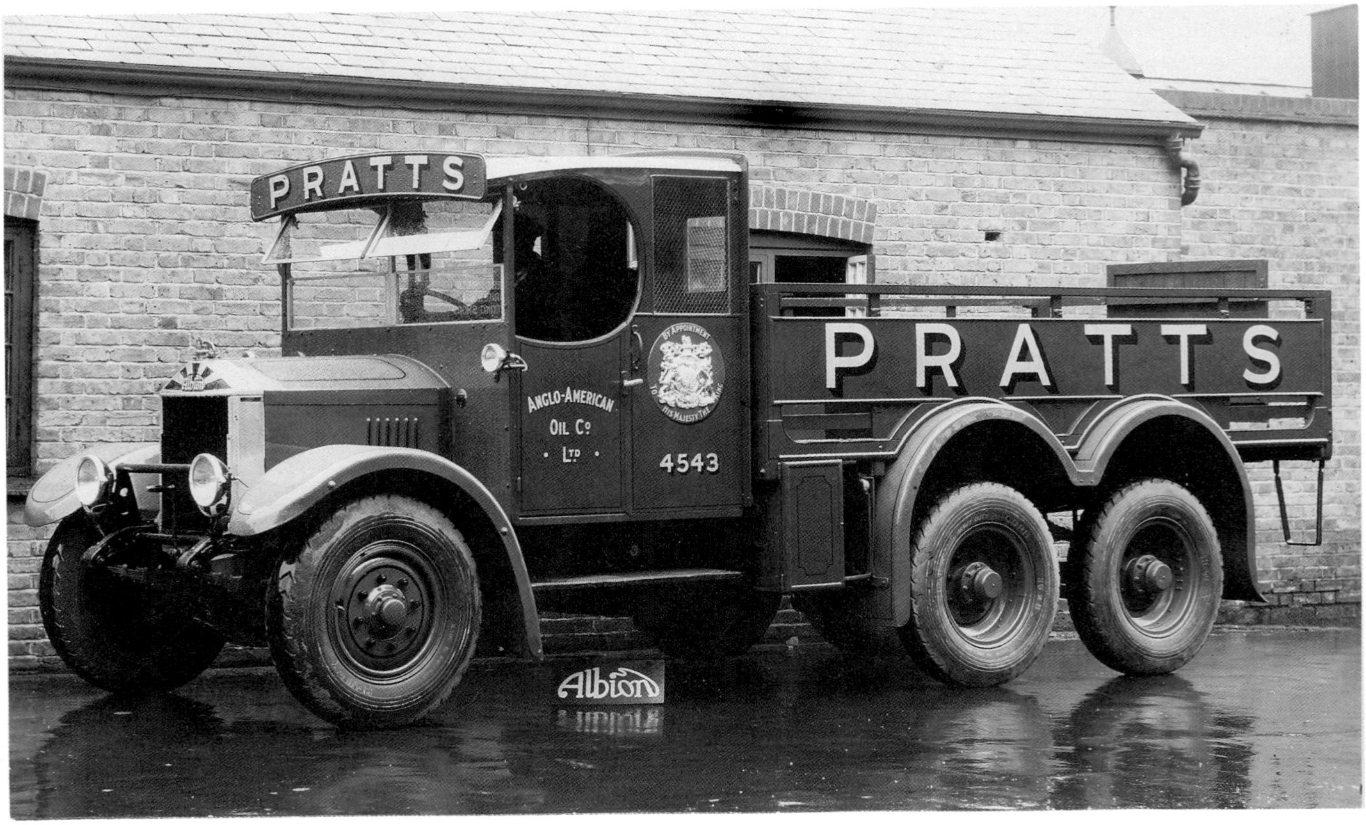
PRATTS
PRATTS
ANGLO-AMERICAN
OIL Co
LTD
4543
Albion

South Africa became an important market for Albion and members of the Blackwood Murray family ultimately settled there. This is an 80 bhp Albion-Merryweather for Pretoria able to pump 550 gpm at 125 psi or up to 850 gpm at 50 psi. The machine still exists and is currently being restored. Its tapered chassis is similar to that of the 30/60 passenger chassis.

Left: The Model 31 of the late 1920s and early 1930s was a three/four ton 6 x 4 lorry for arduous on and off-road use. The military type with temporary rear wheel tracks on the running board was for the Australian Defence Force, whilst Pratts' need for an off-road capability is harder to define. As it appears to be built to Petroleum Regulations it is presumably not for overseas oilfield exploration. Note the high clearance rear wings on both vehicles, made necessary by the WD-pattern central trunnion mounted suspension that allowed maximum wheel-to-ground contact in rough country.

" Clyde-built " is the hall mark of a really first-class engineering product. The new Canadian Pacific Liner " Empress of Britain," and the Albion are both Clyde-built. Each in its class is a supreme example of the finest engineering in the world.

"CLYDE-BUILT"

ALBION MOTOR CAR CO., LTD., SCOTSTOUN, GLASGOW.

Also at London, Leeds, Sheffield, Manchester, Bristol & Birmingham.

1931 saw the arrival of a new family of Albion psv chassis called the Valkyrie, Valiant and Victor. The Valkyrie seated 32-36 passengers and had a six-cylinder 120 bhp petrol engine, though diesel versions were soon offered. The one shown here has a William Arnold body built in Manchester. The engine had dry liners, aluminium pistons and a high camshaft that operated bell crank rockers acting direct on the horizontal valves, which were on the opposite side of the block to the sparking plugs.

A splendid advertisement from Albion in April 1931 comparing the Clyde-built Viking to the Empress of Britain. Despite the optimism, this was a desperately difficult period for the Glasgow region with the Great Depression biting into most of the local industries. The mighty Beardmore lorry, taxi, railway, ship and aircraft firm was tottering, Albion's early rivals, Halley, had just been taken over and virtually all the other commercial vehicle firms had disappeared.

Overleaf: This February 1932 advertisement shows the Model 70 Valiant, which had a smaller 85 bhp version of the Valkyrie's engine and, like it, was intended for 32-36 passengers. The copy makes a virtue of the by then out-dated separate gearbox layout, though the valve gear already described was a boon if you wanted to remove the cylinder head.

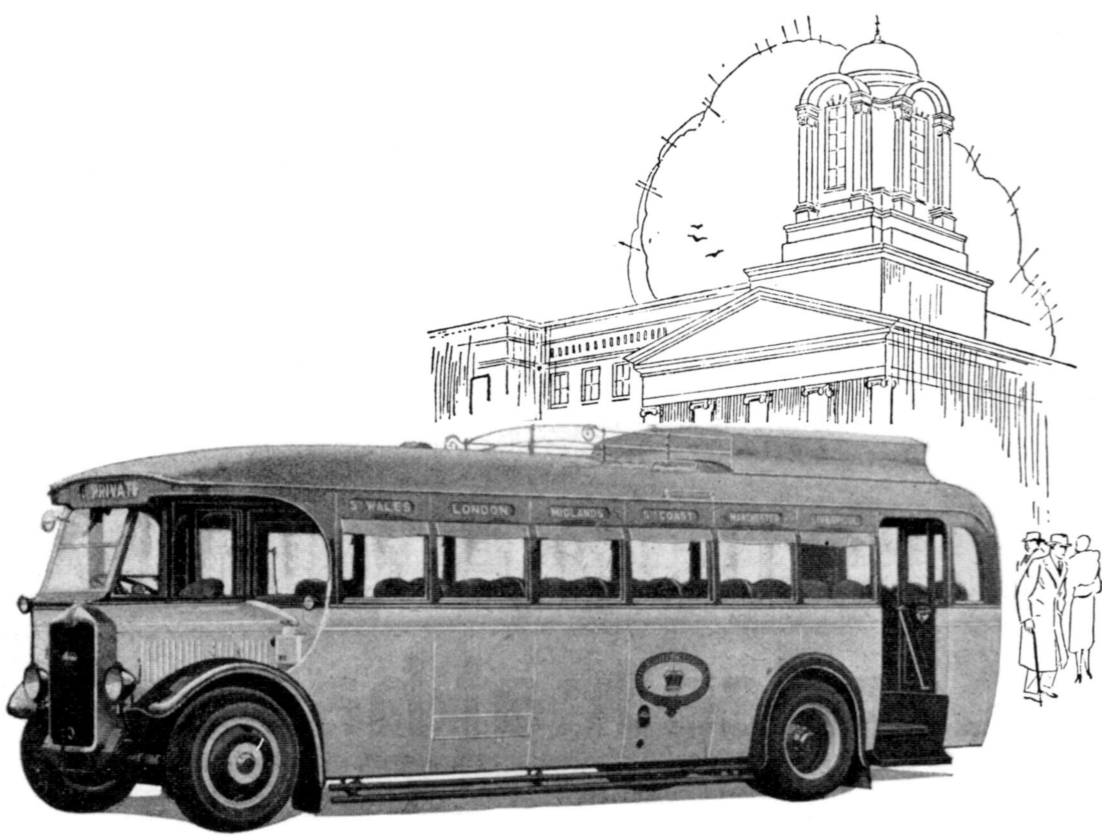

How and why the Albion "Valiant" reduces maintenance costs—

1. The cylinders and crankcase form a single casting of great rigidity, ensuring increased life of bearings.
2. The special high-camshaft design permits decarbonising without disturbance of valve timing.
3. The gearbox being mounted separately from the engine makes both units easier to handle and simplifies clutch maintenance.
4. All brakes can be relined without disturbing the hub bearings.
5. The accessibility of the chassis is unsurpassed.

MAY WE SEND A DEMONSTRATION MODEL FOR YOUR INSPECTION ?

ALBION MOTORS LTD.
SCOTSTOUN, GLASGOW, W.4
London : Bank Buildings, 20 Kingsway, W.C.2.
Also at Manchester, Leeds, Sheffield, Birmingham, Bristol and now at Edinburgh.

Albion

TALKING OF ECONOMY — ALBION IS THE LAST WORD

The Model 34 five-tonner was offered between 1927 and 1933 and was Albion's largest goods model of the time. This one dates from 1930 and has a relatively early example of an underbody ram hydraulic tipper. The engine was a 34 hp four-cylinder petrol unit.

Both four- and six-cylinder versions of Albion's six-tonner of 1932 onwards were available. Judging by the long bonnet this is a six-cylinder type working for Harrods with a drawbar trailer from 1933. Note the railway containers that it is carrying and the set-back front axle that was a popular feature at the time, both for manoeuvrability and weight distribution.

52/120 H.P. 6-CYLINDER PETROL ENGINE

Bore - - - -	$4\frac{5}{8}''$	R.A.C. rating -	51.3 H.P.
Stroke - - - -	$5\frac{1}{2}''$	B.H.P. at 2,200 r.p.m.	120

The cylinders are of cast iron formed in a single block, rigidly attached to the aluminium crankcase. Renewable dry liners are pressed into the cylinders and the exhaust valve seats are also inserted. The overhead valves are carried in the two detachable cylinder heads and are actuated by push rods and rockers, the camshaft being carried high up in the offside of the cylinder block. The heads can thus be removed without disturbing the camshaft drive, or altering the valve timing. Pistons may be withdrawn through the top. The engine is lubricated by forced feed. Filtered oil is delivered under pressure to the seven main bearings and thence to the big end bearings, while oil is also led to the camshaft bearings and valve rockers. The cylinder walls are lubricated by splash. The fan is positively driven from the timing chain through a friction clutch, and the water pump, driven in tandem with the dynamo on the nearside of the engine, is of the carbon gland type requiring no adjustment by the operator. Battery and coil ignition with automatic advance and retard, is fitted as standard. The distributor is on the nearside of the engine and is driven by skew gear from the timing chain. Magneto ignition can be fitted alternatively at extra charge. The fully automatic carburettor with hot spot induction ensures efficiency, economy, and flexibility under all conditions. The petrol feed is by Amal pump, actuated by a cam on the distributor driving shaft.

52/105 H.P. 6-CYLINDER OIL ENGINE

Bore - - - -	$4\frac{5}{8}''$	R.A.C. rating -	51.3 H.P.
Stroke - - -	$5\frac{1}{2}''$	B.H.P. at 1,800 r.p.m.	105

The 6-cylinder Albion Oil Engine works on the direct injection system. The cylinders are of cast iron formed in a single block, rigidly attached to the aluminium crankcase. Renewable dry liners are pressed into the cylinders. The overhead valves, which are quite plain and not locked in any particular position, are carried in the two detachable cylinder heads, and are actuated by push rods and rockers, the camshaft being carried high up in the offside of the cylinder block. The heads can thus be removed without disturbing the camshaft drive or valve timing. The inlet ports are designed to give a controlled degree of swirl. Lubrication is by forced feed. Filtered oil is delivered under pressure to the seven main bearings and thence to the big end bearings, while oil is also delivered to the camshaft bearings and valve rockers. The cylinder walls are lubricated by splash. The fan is positively driven from the timing chain through a friction clutch, and the water pump, driven in tandem with the dynamo on the nearside of the engine, is of the carbon gland type requiring no adjustment by the operator. The fuel pump and injectors are of the CAV-Bosch type and the governor incorporated in the pump limits the minimum and maximum engine speeds to 400 r.p.m. and 1,850 r.p.m. respectively. A rotary exhauster is driven in tandem with the fuel pump on the nearside of the engine. The fuel feed pump is driven from the Bosch pump camshaft. The fuel system incorporates no less than three efficient filters, thus ensuring that only clean fuel reaches the pump and injectors. An electric starter is included which, with the decompressor gear, ensures easy starting under all conditions.

The death of Dr. Blackwood Murray delayed Albion's diesel engine development, though by the end of 1933 many of the heavier models could have an Albion diesel. Until then, and indeed subsequently, some models could be had with Dorman, Beardmore or Gardner diesels. Beardmore diesels were used for a Glasgow Corporation fleet order in 1935. Here we see a comparison between the Albion oil (diesel) and petrol engines available in the Valkyrie.

An October 1934 advertisement showing three sizes of Albion bus. The Victor was the only one without a diesel (heavy oil) engine option, though one was later available, and could be had with forward or normal control. Prior to the relatively widespread use of the Venturer double decker, Albion had tried the 56/60-passenger Valorous but had sold very few examples. Some Venturers went to Sydney Transport Board, where, for a time, they were the only double deckers in Australia.

During the brief popularity of the rigid six-wheeler bus in the 1930s Albion catered for the demand with the 49 hp six-cylinder PW145 for 39/40 passengers and the PR145 40/44-seater, which had a 34 hp engine. This Highland six-wheeler dates from 1935 and is shown in later life. The first mention of an Albion six-wheel psv in *Commercial Motor* came early in 1936, when it was referred to simply as a Valkyrie six-wheeler.

Two important events to Albion were the granting of a Royal Warrant early in 1934 as suppliers of lorries to King George V on his estate at Balmoral (followed by another in 1940 in the reign of George VI), and the arrival of the Model 127 in 1935. This 5½ tonner (the load plus body and cab) weighed under 2½ tons and as a result was permitted to travel at 30 mph. It had a four-cylinder 65 bhp petrol engine with four-speed gearbox, overhead worm axle and triple servo four-wheel brakes. The brick and tile lorry from Sileby is a typical example, whilst the 1936 fleet of tippers may be the broadly similar lightweight six-tonners. They, incidentally, cost £103 15s 0d (£103.75) each to body and paint at Goddard's of Oadby.

BY APPOINTMENT

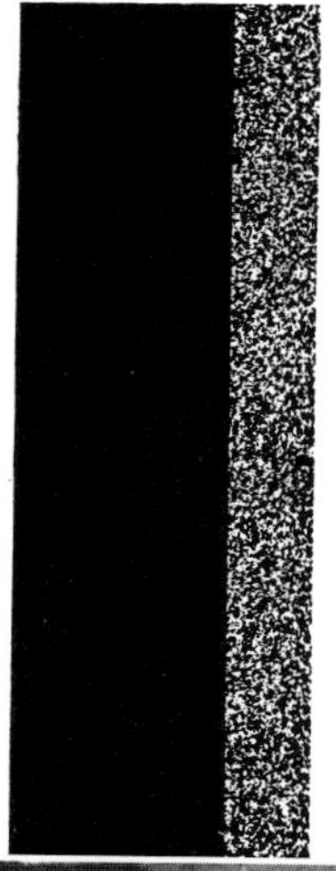

ALBION

30 M.P.H.

5½ TON CHASSIS

MODEL 127 OVERTYPE

GROSS LOAD 122 CWTS.

(13,664 POUNDS)

ALBION MOTORS LIMITED

SCOTSTOUN . . . . GLASGOW, W.4

LONDON . . . . . . Bank Buildings, 20 Kingsway, W.C.2

MANCHESTER, 670 Chester Road, Old Trafford, 16
LEEDS ... ... 39/41 Camp Road, 7
LINCOLN ... ... 10 Mint Street
BIRMINGHAM ... ... 98 Livery Street, 3
BRISTOL ... ... Booth Road Bedminster 3

LIVERPOOL, 33 Imperial Chambers, 62 Dale St., 2
SHEFFIELD ... ... Beulah Road Owlerton, 6
NOTTINGHAM, Rutland Chambers, St. Peter's Gate
NORWICH ... ... 16 Thorpe Road
EDINBURGH, Dunedin Street (off Beaverhall Road), 7

BELFAST ... ... 43a Smithfield

L 413

W.T.WRIGHT & Co LTD
BRICK & TILE MANUFACTURERS
SILE
Nr LOUGHBOROUGH.
SPEED 20 M.P.H.

FOSSE HAULAGE Co LTD HASTINGS ROAD LEICESTER
PHONE 27736
12
ARY 543
13
ARY 545
14
ARY 544

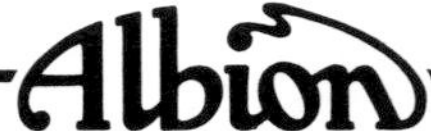

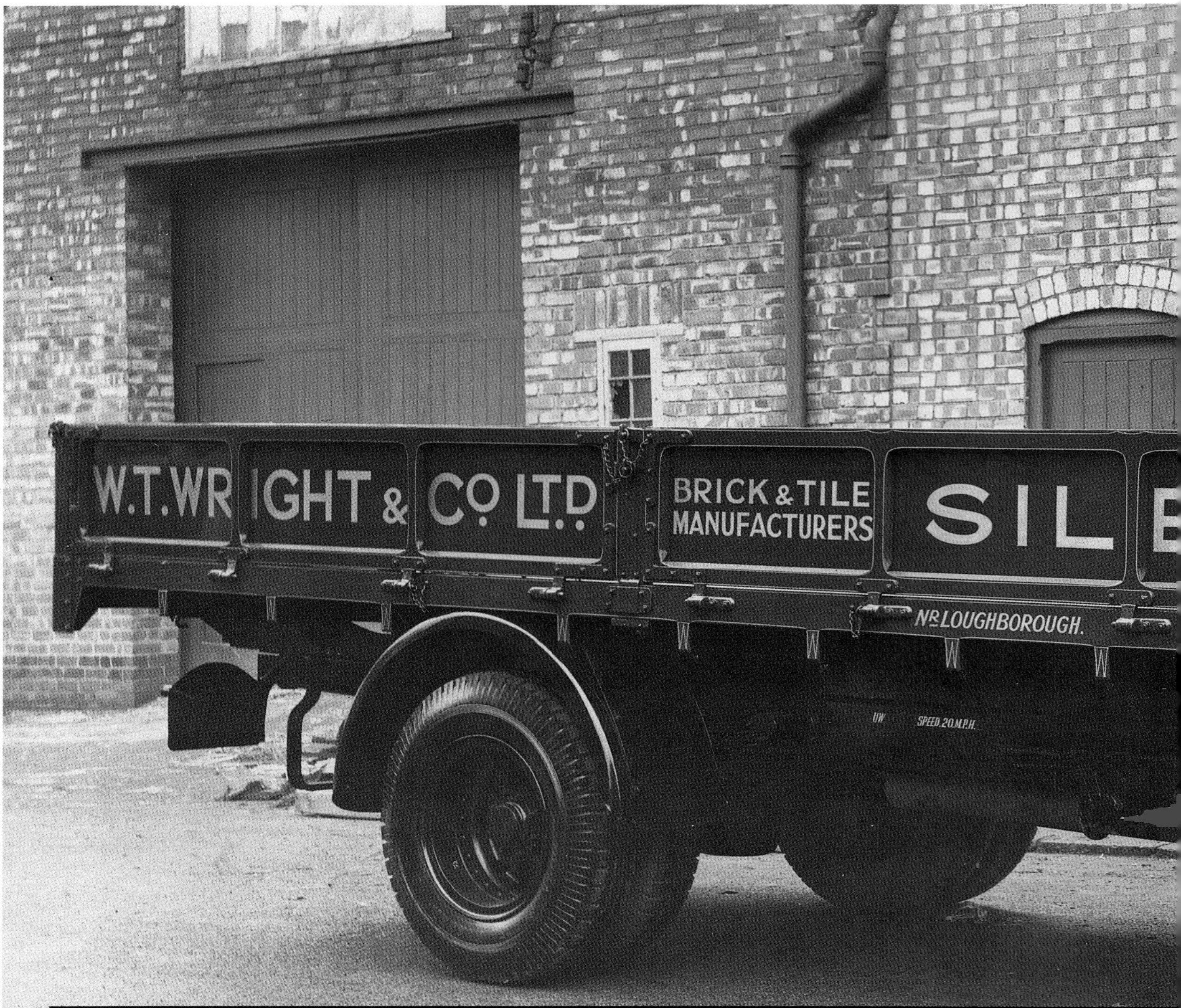

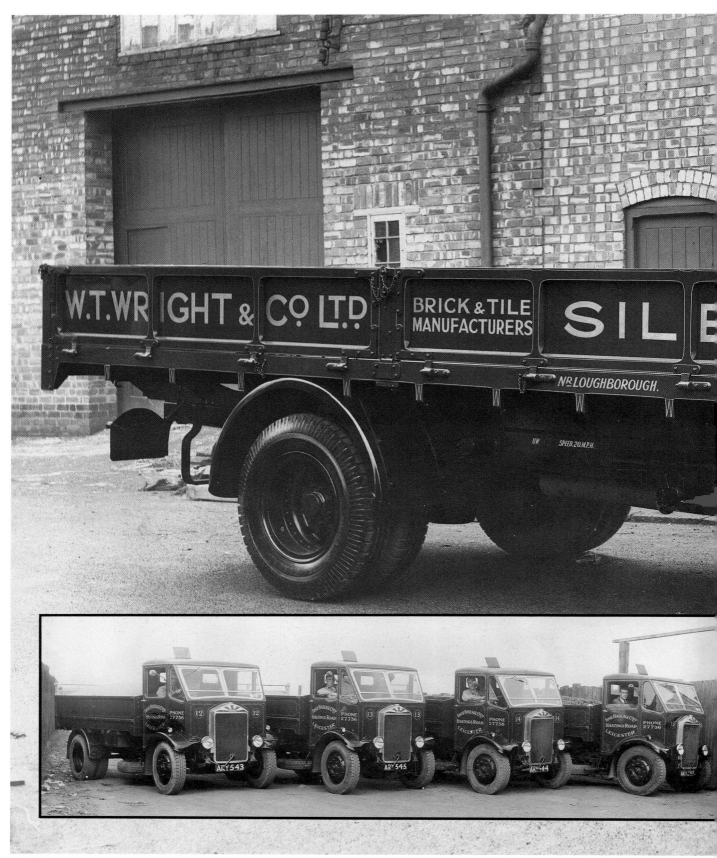

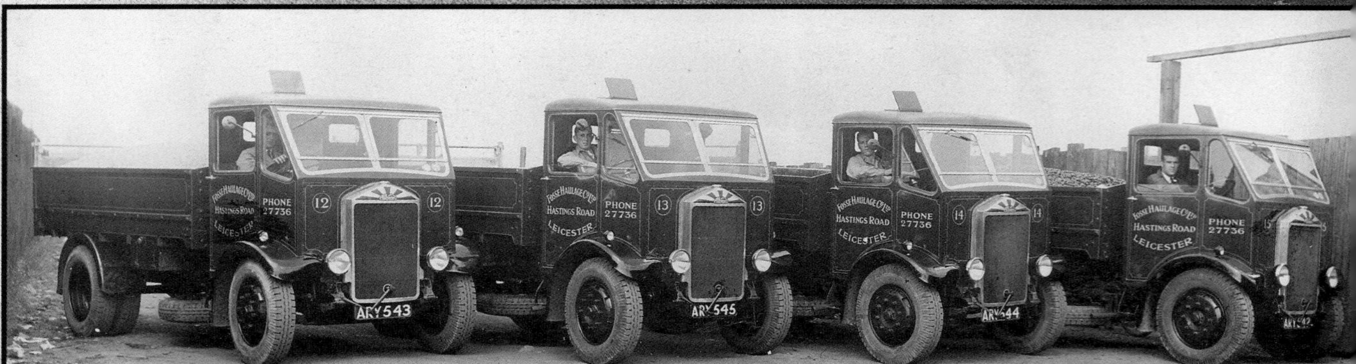

BY

Another Albion bodied by Goddard at Oadby. This is a petrol engined normal control $3^1/_2/4$ tonner. Albion's conservative styling belied its lightweight construction and advanced engineering in the 1930s. Another normal control model, about which little information is recorded, is the Drysdale equipped fire appliance shown at the Albion Works (possibly the new repair section in the former Halley Works taken over in 1935).

Another view at the Works with a 3/3½ ton chassis parked outside and used to demonstrate its brake operating mechanism. The firm was by then known as Albion Motors Ltd., though the old "Motor Car" title can just be read on the wall.

It is difficult to date this Model RL59 with any accuracy as Wigtown was not a prolific licenser of vehicles and the numbers on this one are impossible to decipher. The imposing lorry was fitted with a Gardner 6LW and was a model that was new in Spring 1934. The R and RL59 were rated as ten to twelve-tonners and were Albion's first heavy duty six-wheelers. A six- to seven-ton four-wheel version with this cab and front axle layout was also available from late 1933. At this time Albion employed 1,650 men in Glasgow and a further 300 at depots around the British Isles.

An interesting contrast between one of the last Halleys (4398) and a contemporary Albion tanker (5854). The Albion dates from 1934, the year in which the North British Locomotive Co. Ltd. decided that after seven years of mounting losses at Halley its fifty per cent holding was doomed. The final Halleys had Halley-Ricardo petrol engines or Perkins diesels. When Albion acquired the Yoker factory in 1935, as a spares and service headquarters, they took no further interest in their former rivals and Halley's tooling went to the 600 Group, who sold the spares and goodwill on to R.H. Collier in Birmingham. Later Albion was to use some of Halley's old model names, life Chieftain.

In its early days Halley (which as we saw started in a former Albion workshop) had been a serious threat to Albion and probably produced more vehicles for a time before the Great War. However, the premature death of George Halley soon after the Great War and the firm's enthusiasm for six cylinders at a time when haulage men thought this spelled decadence, seriously weakened it. It seems fitting to pay our respects to Halley and here we see a c.1912 dropside from its strongest period, a mid 'twenties artic tanker, an advertisement for municipal models in 1931 and a view inside the Yoker works that includes a Halley Neptune double decker on tilt test.

NOTABLE HALLEYS

Below is illustrated a fleet of four Municipal Cleansing Vehicles recently supplied to the Birmingham Corporation. Two 1,000-gallon Street Watering and Sprinkling Machines mounted on Halley No. "E.F.21" Forward Control 4-ton Chassis and two 500-gallon Vacuum Gully and Cesspool Emptying Machines mounted on Halley "W.21" Chassis.

Above we show the 1,000 gallon Street Watering and Sprinkling Machine of which only the front view is shown in the first photograph.

◇

Here are two views of one of a fleet of six Tramway Tower Waggons which have just been supplied to the Glasgow Corporation Transport Department.

The photograph, which shows a Halley Tower Waggon in action, demonstrates the ease and adaptability of the equipment.

LIST PRICES (ex Works) of Halley Goods Carrying Vehicles on pneumatic tyres with spare wheel and tyre :-

Model.	Load.	Control.	Wheelbase.	Price.
W20	40 cwt.	Normal	12′0″	£495
W21	50 cwt.	Semi-Forward	12′0″	£530x
Talisman	50 cwt.	Normal	14′3″	£575
DF2	60 cwt.	Normal	12′1″&13′4″	£610
P9H	80 cwt.	Normal	12′0″&13′4″	£815xx
EF21	80 cwt.	Forward	11′0″&12′6″	£840xx
EF20	100 cwt.	Normal	14′6″	£895xx
EF21	100 cwt.	Forward	11′0″&12′6″	£905xx

Prices of rigid six wheeled vehicles for 8-10 Tons load on application.

X—Pneumatic Front, Solid Rear, Low Loading Refuse Collection Tipping Chassis.
XX—Includes Front Mudwings and Electric Lighting Set.

We are specialists in the manufacture of Street Cleansing Machines, Gully and Cesspool Emptying Machines, tank vehicles of all descriptions for Municipal and Public Authorities.

Submit your problems to us and we will willingly furnish designs to meet your difficulties.

HALLEY MOTORS LTD

Associated with the NORTH BRITISH LOCOMOTIVE Co. Ltd.

LONDON DEPOT :
195, Clapham Road, S.W. 9.

: YOKER :
GLASGOW

MANCHESTER DEPOT :
Altrincham Street, London Rd.

In 1935, when the Scotstoun factory covered ten acres, Albion exceeded all its previous production records, a success due in part to a highly buoyant export trade. A few of its recent orders had included 13 Valkyries to Kenya, 75 to Bombay and 137 small buses with Dorman engines and Park Royal bodies to HEH the Nizam State Railway Board. Shown here is a M34 four-tonner plus several trailers operated by Victoria Falls and Transvaal Power Co. Ltd. of Johannesburg.

As well as moving up the weight range Albion continued to do good business with its 30/40 cwt. types. These had 20 hp four-cylinder petrol engines and were virtually indestructable. Here we see a 500 gallon forward control tanker and more typical bonnetted examples of the mid 1930s. They were the backbone of numerous distribution fleets, not least the Fry's chocolate factory which ran at least forty.

'S
TEACHER'S
The Whisky of the Good Old Days
ESTAB. 1830
32/3, COWCROSS ST
LONDON, E.C.1.
& GLASGOW.

UNIVERSAL BOTTLING Co Ltd
371
TELEPHONE 2627 AMHERST
UNIVERSAL
BOTTLING Co Ltd
DUV 478

CLARK HUNT & Co Ltd
MIDDLESEX IRON WORKS.
PHONE BISHOPSGATE 2131 (11 LINES)
159-160-161, SHOREDITCH,
LONDON, E.1.
378
WHOLESALE IRONMONGERS
IRON & STEEL MERCHANTS

A random selection of mid 1930s types including a 1935 LCA 44 2/2½ tonner operated by Shuttleworth's, a firm still in the timber business, a heavier dropside (probably a 127) of the same year, and a fire appliance new to Surrey in 1937 that was still in service twenty years later (the other vehicles shown in the 1950s are a Dennis and a modern Commer).

This CX.4N chassis for East London Municipality in South Africa had a tower that could be extended from 13 to 25 feet and an extra cabin for equipment and staff. It was powered by Albion's EN 24 9.1 litre six-cylinder diesel with a four available as an alternative. Albion's original 1933 diesel had been extensively redesigned by the Ricardo consultancy in the following year but did not become a commercial success until later in the 1930s, a further redesign having been necessary in 1937. The CX chassis models first appeared at the 1937 Commercial Motor Show.

Early in 1937 Albion filled the last major gap in its range when it announced the T561 12/13 ton capacity rigid eight. This was available with a 110 bhp Albion six-cylinder magneto ignition petrol engine as standard and a Gardner 6LW as an option. The example shown here dates from early 1938 and had servo brakes on all but the second steered axle. Four- or five-speed gearboxes were available and double overhead worm drive was standard. An improved eight-wheeler in the new CX family arrived early in 1938 for 15 ton loads and the Venturer bus also joined the CX range that year with in-unit engine and gearbox.

The CX 27, new in June 1938, was a twin steer ten-tonner with the same engine options as the eight-wheeler and in-unit four- or five-speed gearbox. It was braked on all wheels. The complete vehicle towing a trailer dates from 1939 and is shown at work with air raid precaution lamp blackout masks. The wings are painted white to aid visibility for other road users.

The all-Albion fleet of Stewart Bros of Arbroath, photographed in the later 1930s. Over to the right are some early solid tyred models, whilst the rest get progressively more modern and end with a 1932 type on the left. The Stewart fleet passed into British Road Services soon after the Second World War.

London County Council Tramways, and then London Transport, bought a number of forward and normal control Albions in the 1930s for track laying and maintenance. This is believed to be one of them on test. The crane was worked by a gearbox power take-off and the Heath Robinson arrangement on the front is probably to stabilise the vehicle when lifting heavy side loads.

Albion

Some more examples of Albion's very popular 127 model. The Rowe Bros five-tonner was new in 1938 and the one on hire to Nidderdale Quarries dates from a year earlier. The two with Watkins Transport of West Bromwich were new in 1937 and look decidedly archaic when compared to the American Diamond T of 1938 with British cab alongside them.

NIDDERDALE QUARRIES LTD.
PATELEY BRIDGE.
Crushed Lime Stone & Tar Macadam.
MYERS' GARAGE,
Haulage Contractors,
DARLEY,
HARROGATE.

WATKINS TRANSPORT LTD
Phone West Brom 0138
EA8268
EA 9213

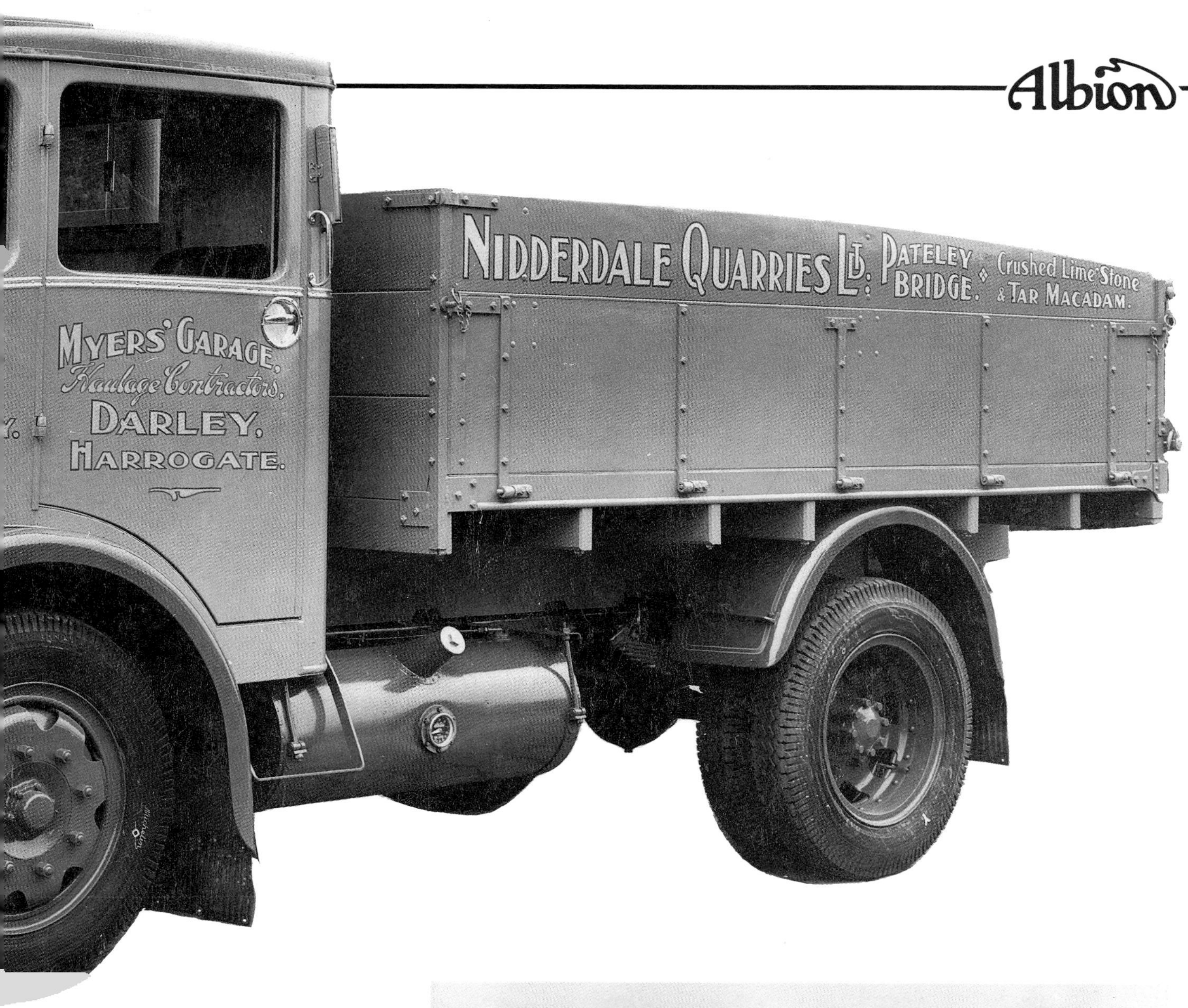

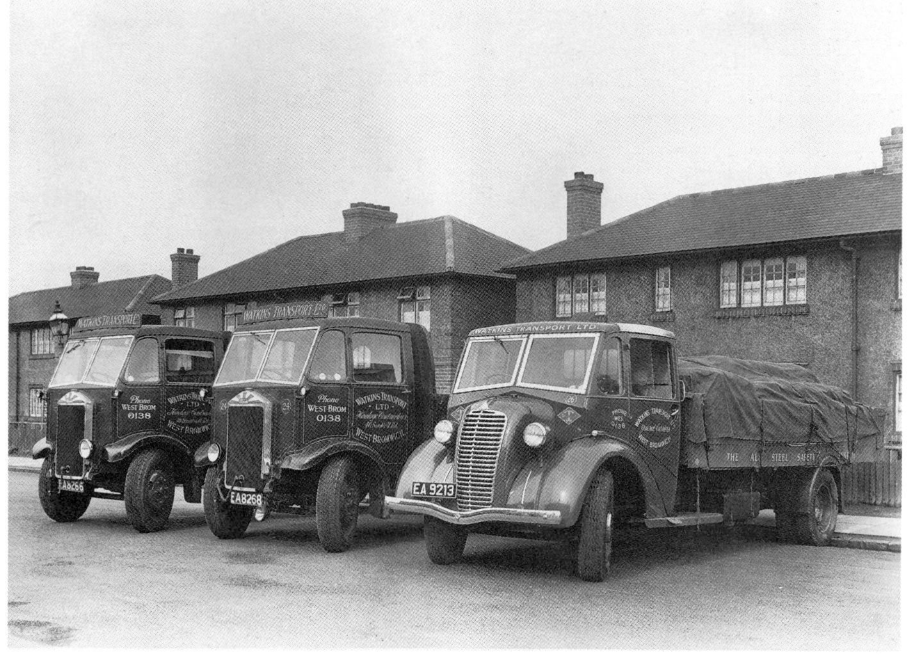

AA Motor Services owned the 1938 registered Valkyrie with the "sure as sunrise" motif cleverly painted on the radiator mesh as well as on the enamelled radiator badge. Bodywork was by R.Y. Pickering and Co. Ltd. of Wishaw.

The advertisement for the lighter Victor dates from February 1937.

The doubledeck Venturer was a CX19 model new to United Welsh in 1938. Reference to the municipal fleet list of that year shows Albion with very few stongholds. Even Glasgow had only 20 Albions compared with 435 Leylands, 52 AEC and 25 Daimlers. Edinburgh had only one Albion.

Though Albion's heyday as a fire appliance chassis manufacturer had passed, its mechanical components were often used by Merryweather of Greenwich. This 1941 scene in Farringdon Street is by courtesy of London Fire Brigade. As well as showing several trailer pumps it features a Merryweather escape in the background.

A variation on the 30 cwt. theme was the RAF ambulance first built in 1934, though AM463 dates from 1937. It was one of two hundred similar vehicles and was abandoned after the Dunkirk evacuation and then rescued years later by Richard Robinson of Potters Bar for preservation. Note that it has Gruss air springs attached to the front spring eyes in an effort to smooth out some of the worst undulations when being driven fast on give-and-take surfaces.

Albion built a wide assortment of vehicles during the Second World War, including nearly two thousand 30 cwt. types used for all manner of duties from ambulance to 350 gallon refueller. The 127 model was also important in military and civilian roles and from February 1940 there was also a 4 x 4 three-ton version known as the FT11. Shown here is one of its three-ton 6 x 6 models, built originally as a low silhouette Field Artillery Tractor with Turner eight-ton winch, and a 6 x 4 field X-ray unit in wartime service.

A passenger chassis for overseas conditions –

Albion 'Viking' 48-passenger bus for use in South Africa.

The ALBION 'VIKING'

Embodying all that 49 years' experience in Export Markets has taught us, the Albion 'Viking' chassis is specially designed to meet the needs of the overseas operator.

With the traditional Albion reputation for reliability and exceptional economy of operation it is powered by the well-tried 52/120 H.P. Albion 6-cylinder oil engine, and is available with 18′ 3″ or 20′ 6″ wheelbase to suit 30′ 0″ or 33′ 0″ overall vehicle lengths respectively and an overall width of 8′ 0″.

Albion's heavy export single decker was the six-cylinder Viking shown here in a June 1949 advertisement. For lighter work there was the Victor FT.39AN shown here with Mulliner's 35-seat bodywork for use in Sierra Leone. The home version of the Viking was the six-cylinder Valiant shown here in a December 1949 advertisement. Finally, there is a 1949 advertisement for another Victor, showing it at use in the Albion stronghold of Jersey. The Victor was unusual in making do with only four cylinders when used with the engine from the Chieftain lorry, though a petrol six was also offered.

SAFETY
COMFORT
ECONOMY

THE ALBION
VALIANT

A "Valiant" in the service of a Yorkshire operator.

Designed essentially for coach and heavy duty bus service, where maximum road performance and economy of operation are of primary consideration, the "Valiant" is the choice of discerning operators. Powered by the smooth running 120 b.h.p. 6-cylinder Albion direct injection oil engine, the chassis can accommodate bodywork seating up to a maximum of 36 passengers within the requirements of the Ministry of Transport Regulations.

Also at Manchester, Leeds, Sheffield, Hull, Lincoln, Nottingham, Birmingham, Bristol, Edinburgh and Belfast

An Outstanding Achievement –

The Albion 'Victor'

One of a fleet of 'Victors' operated in the Channel Islands by Jersey Motor Transport Co. Ltd.

Before deciding what new vehicles to add to your fleet next season it will pay you to investigate the 'Victor' passenger chassis—an engineering achievement which maintains the great Albion reputation for economical running, smooth performance, safety, freedom from breakdown and durability.

Powerful 75 b.h.p. 4-cyl. Albion oil engine with 5-speed gearbox.
Straight frame and overhead worm drive.
Long flexible road springs with hydraulic shock absorbers front and rear.
Curved dash for modern full-fronted body-work.
Overall dimensions 26' 0" long x 7' 6" wide.
Full 24-volt lighting and starting equipment.
Also available is 'Victor' model with 80 b.h.p. 6-cyl. Albion petrol engine.

EASTER 1950

Delivery of a limited number of 'Victor' chassis can be made in time to permit the mounting of coachwork for Easter traffic.

Also at Manchester, Leeds, Sheffield, Hull, Lincoln, Nottingham, Birmingham, Bristol, Edinburgh, and Belfast.

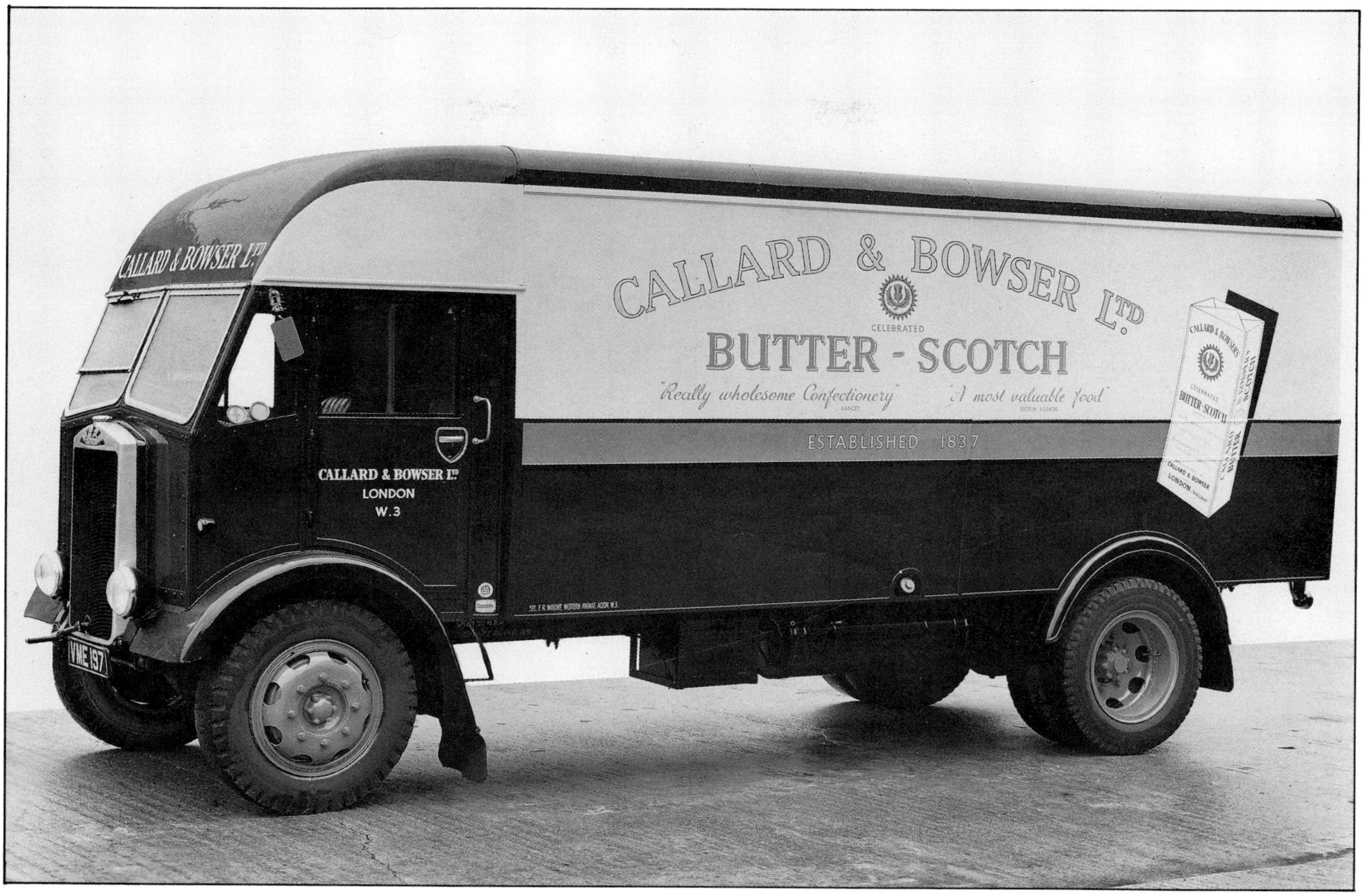

In 1948 Albion improved the old 127 Model and gave it a brand new 75 bhp four-cylinder diesel engine. To signify the change they borrowed the Chieftain model name from Halley's past. The result was an extremely robust, straightforward and frugal 5/6 ton lorry that was to have a major impact on the transport scene. A bonnetted export version was also offered. Shown here are 1949 vans for the Post Office and Callard & Bowser with bodywork by Cunard.

The 75 bhp engine used by the Victor and Chieftain developed its peak power at 2000 rpm and bristled with interesting features. It had automatic variable injection timing which gave it a very flat torque curve and a patented bypass valve in the induction system that obviated the need for an exhauster for the vacuum brakes. Other features included an inertia damper on the propshaft and ingenious flexible mounting of the engine. The Victor and some lorry applications had the silencer bolted straight to the engine so that flexible couplings could be avoided.

The Clydesdale was for twelve tons gross and used the same engine as the Chieftain with a similar five-speed gearbox. It would seem hopelessly underpowered by today's standards, but could cope with the 20 mph speed limit then prevalent for heavy vehicles. The Shell tanker dates from 1950 whilst the heavy duty export tipper photograph was inexplicably stamped "Maudslay Publicity Department". Maudslay had recently joined AEC and Crossley and was perhaps having a close look at its rivals.

There was still a small market for vehicles with large petrol engines. Most of Albion's had magneto ignition, through the 1930s, but by now had the coil and distributor type shown here on this 54/145 hp. It had aluminium pistons, forced feed lubrication and a Zenith carburettor.

Right: This was Albion's rigid eight of 1949 known as the CX79 with 120 bhp diesel. For some reason the eight leggers did not get a model name, even when they were revised in 1950 in the HD two- and three-axle series.

Dekaloy on the number plate was an advertising reminder that the floor of the Bonallack body was made from this light non-slip material.

The HD (heavy duty) artic was in use in Rhodesia and South Africa at the time and, to allow a double shift of drivers, had an early example of sleeper cab.

Glasgow Corporation continued to be a loyal buyer of the Venturer bus, this example from 1946 having Scottish Aviation 56 seat bodywork. This was of fully light alloy construction and was joined to the chassis via Dural cross-members riding on Ferodo pads.

A STOUT LORRY

Under 3-tons unladen weight, legal speed 30 m.p.h. —an impressive 5-ton Albion petrol engined lorry operating in the Liverpool area.

is the Albion 30 M.P.H. 5/6½ tonner

Sturdiness of construction, unequalled length of life, freedom from breakdown, and outstanding economy of operation are the qualities which justify the popularity of the range of 5 and 6½-tons Albion petrol engined chassis. With normal bodywork the unladen weight of a platform lorry can be kept under 3-tons—legal speed 30 m.p.h.

Also available is the "Chieftain" range of 5/6½-ton chassis with Albion oil engine.

Also at Manchester, Leeds, Sheffield, Hull, Lincoln, Nottingham, Birmingham, Bristol, Edinburgh and Belfast.

The Clydesdale of 1950 onwards was at the heavy end of the FT range of four-wheelers. Despite its 12 tons gvw (more in the case of this 2500 gallon artic that worked between Ibadan and Lagos) it made do with Albion's trusty 75 bhp four-cylinder diesel. Above it in the HD range, introduced in 1950, came the six-cylinder 12 ton gross HD53 and several other two-, three- and four-axle models.

At the bottom end of the FT range, which included the Chieftan and Clydesdale, was the petrol engined type shown here. There was also a diesel version called the Clansman for slightly less payload than the smallest Chieftain so this is effectively a petrol Clansman, though judging by this December 1951 advertisement Albion was a bit coy about using the name. Perhaps the infamous Ku Klux variety of Klansman was in the news at the time?

In 1951 Leyland Motors Ltd. started its massive expansion by buying Albion Motors Ltd. Jackson Millar CBE was managing director of Albion at the time, his father having been the early backer of Albion who had then transferred his money into Halley in 1906. Leyland left the Scottish firm alone, though there were some casualties like an interesting 39 seat eight-cylinder pancake engined bus as well as the slow selling Venturer double decker and an experimental horizontally opposed twelve-cylinder 230 bhp engine being developed by Albion in South Africa. The vehicle shown here started life in 1949 as a CX37 coach with 33 seat Burlington body. South Yorkshire Motors needed a double decker in 1957 and in the absence of a Venturer, fitted a Lowbridge body to their old chassis. It eventually passed into preservation with 857,054 miles on the odometer. 1951 was also the year in which Austin and Morris merged. In the case of Leyland and Albion, Leyland in mid year began the exchange of its own six-per-cent cumulative preference stock for the 133,866 six-per-cent Albion preference stock and 597,400 ordinary one-pound shares. The cost to Leyland was almost £3 million.

Albion continued to supply military vehicles in the 1940s and early 1950s, notably 6 x 4 three-ton versions of the Clansman and ten-ton HD 6 x 4 types. Here we see a 1954 HD with 10.45 litre Albion diesel and Jones six ton capacity crane. The recovery vehicle is one of a batch of nine 6 x 6 cargo five-tonners built in 1955/6 with Rolls-Royce eight-cylinder 160 bhp petrol engines. This latter vehicle is still in use, albeit nowadays with a more economical Bedford diesel engine.

To save weight and make their vehicles appear a little more modern some operators specified Holmalloy cabs from the mid 1950s. The Jubilee stout has one of these light alloy cabs built by Holmes (Preston) Ltd. The other two vehicles date from the same period and have traditional Albion cabs. The triple deck sheep container is by Jennings of Sandbach whilst the bullion van for the Commonwealth Bank of Australia is by Longwell Green Coachworks of Bristol.

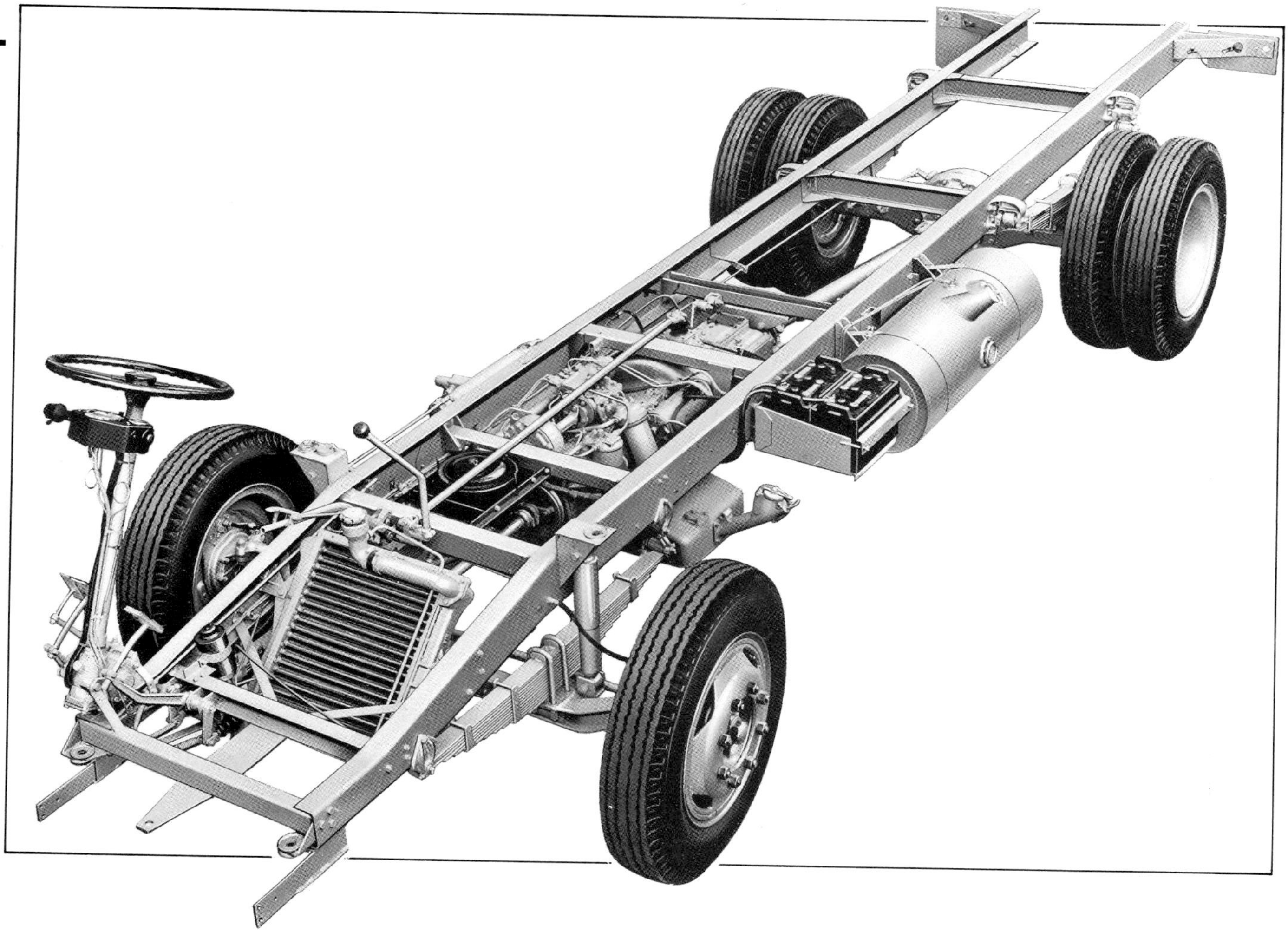

In view of the Leyland takeover it was perhaps a little surprising that Scotstoun was permitted to go ahead with a completely new and unusual design, though admittedly it was in an area not covered by the Leyland range, the under-floor, horizontal engined Claymore 3/4 tonner of 1954. It was built in small numbers with an overhead worm back axle but then in 1958 was revised and simplified. A later CL.3AN four-cylinder horizontal diesel chassis is shown here together with a MR7N brewer's dray of late 1955.

Here we have an assortment of Albion products from the year of 1956. The Caudle's 1,035 cu.ft. pantechnicon is on a Chieftain chassis, whilst the remainder are Clydesdales plus the new six-wheeler version known as the Reiver for ten-ton loads. The HD models had been quietly discontinued in 1955/7 though not before an experimental six-wheel Royal Scott with horizontal 175 bhp diesel had been built, and been replaced by variations on the more lightly built FT theme, available with Albion or Leyland engines. The artic has a Scammell ten-ton trailer, Scammell having joined Albion in the growing Leyland group in 1955. The bonneted 11 tons gross Clydesdale was shown at the 1956 Commercial Motor Show with Albion's own double-skinned steel cab and a 100 bhp Leyland diesel.

BULWARK TRANSPORT
BULWARK TRANSPORT LTD CHIPPENHAM WILTS.
270
OAM 270

SHELL-MEX AND BP LTD
SHELL
PETROLEUM PRODUCTS
BP
SHELL-MEX AND BP LTD
6567 NH
SXC 318

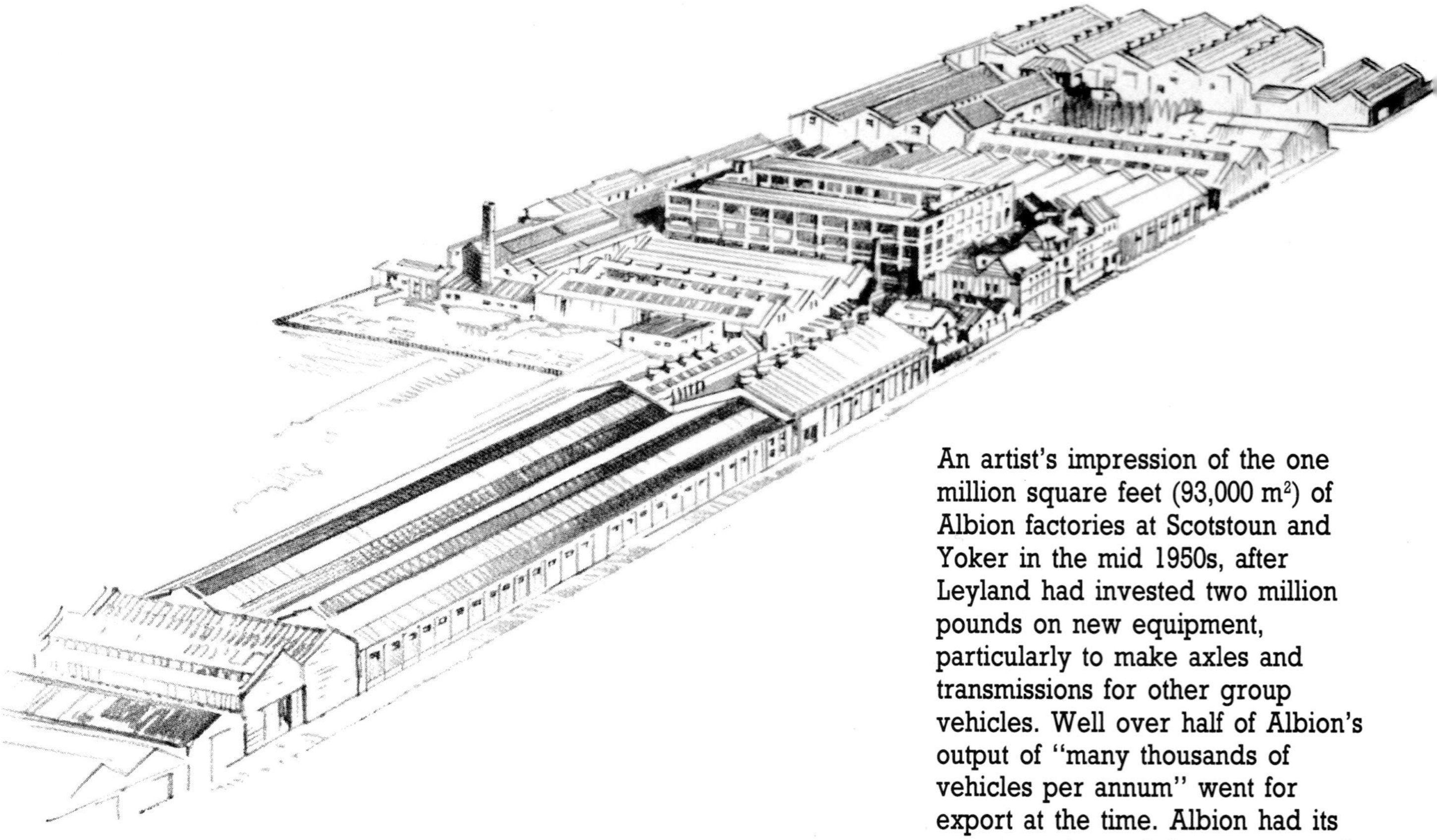

An artist's impression of the one million square feet (93,000 m²) of Albion factories at Scotstoun and Yoker in the mid 1950s, after Leyland had invested two million pounds on new equipment, particularly to make axles and transmissions for other group vehicles. Well over half of Albion's output of "many thousands of vehicles per annum" went for export at the time. Albion had its own experimental department and test track. The conveyor assembly line was 750 feet (228 metres) long.

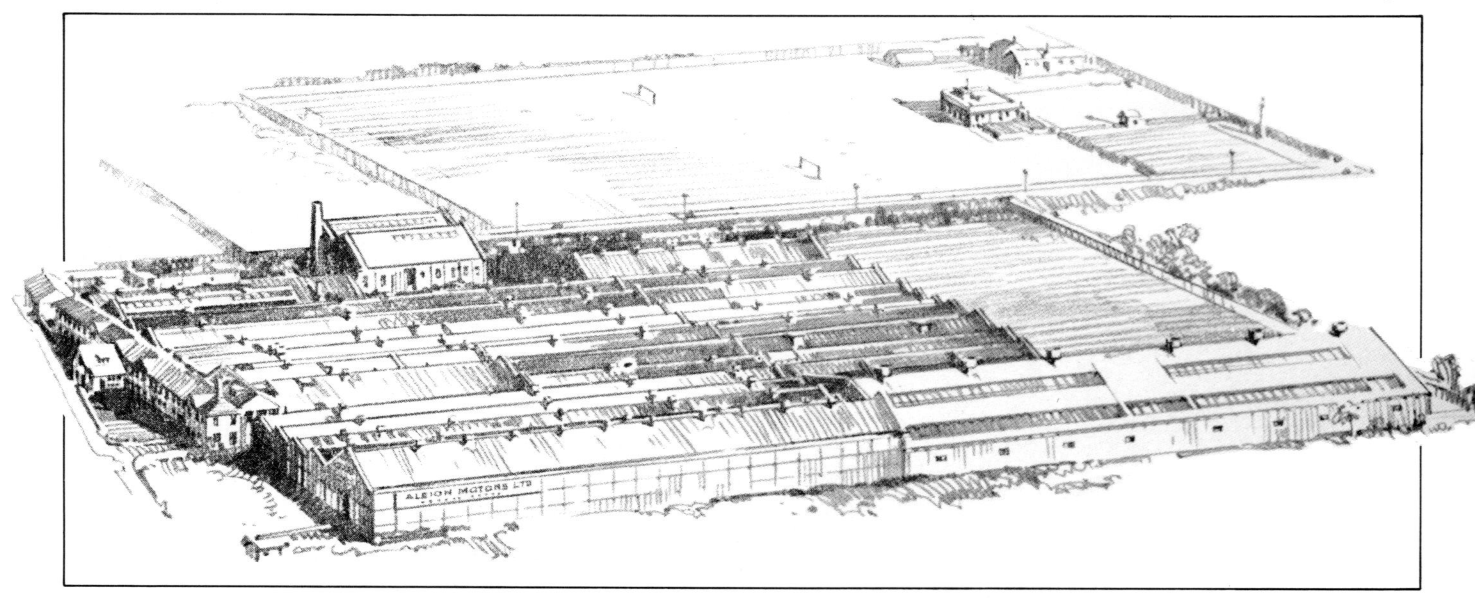

A shortlived lightweight version of the Claymore with its engine derated from 60 to 55 bhp for 30/35 cwt. loads was introduced at the 1955 Scottish Motor Show under the name Cairn. It had the same wheelbase of ten feet as the smallest Claymore and smaller tyres. Shown here is what may well be the only surviving example, seen at a rally in Somerset in 1987.

The Nimbus was the passenger version of the underfloor engined Claymore. Shown is a 1957 MR9N chassis with 60 bhp 3.83 litre engine and Van Hool 31 seat coachwork operating in Holland. Several passenger versions of Albion goods models were soon to join this and the familiar Victor. They included the Viking with front or rear engine, and front engined Clydesdale export model (a 1960 chassis diagram is shown, as well as a left-hand drive chassis in photographic form), as well as the forty seat six-cylinder Aberdonian of the late 1950s.

MODEL	TYRE DATA	FRONT TRACK	REAR TRACK	A	B	C	D	E	F	H
CD23ANW	10·00-20 (12PLY)	6'-7 3/16"	5'-11"	3'-3"	1'-7 1/4"	3'-2 13/16"	1'-6 1/4"	1'-11 1/4"	7'-11 1/2"	7'-10 1/4"
CD23ANW	9·00-20 (12PLY)	6'-7 5/8"	5'-11"	3'-2 3/4"	1'-7 1/4"	3'-2 1/16"	1'-6 1/4"	1'-9 1/4"	7'-11 1/2"	7'-8 1/4"

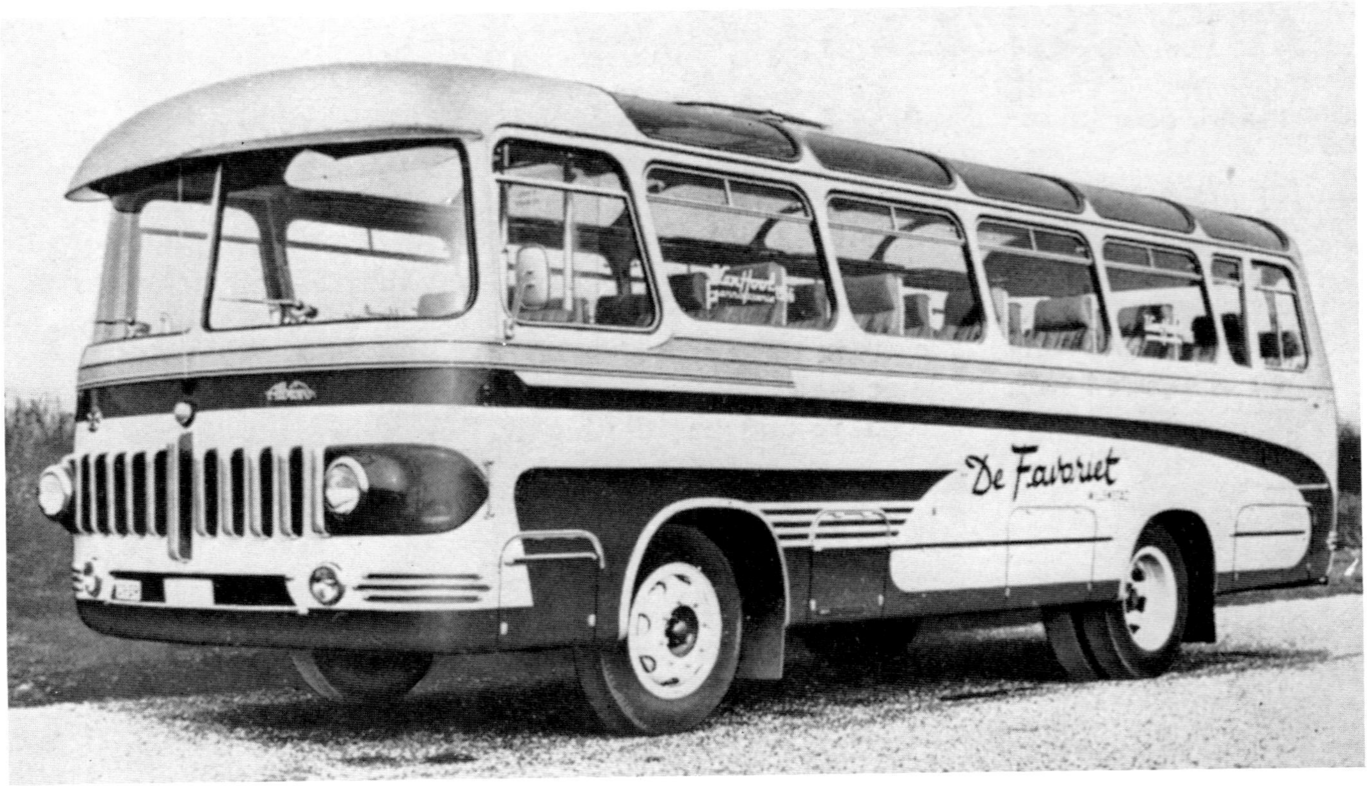

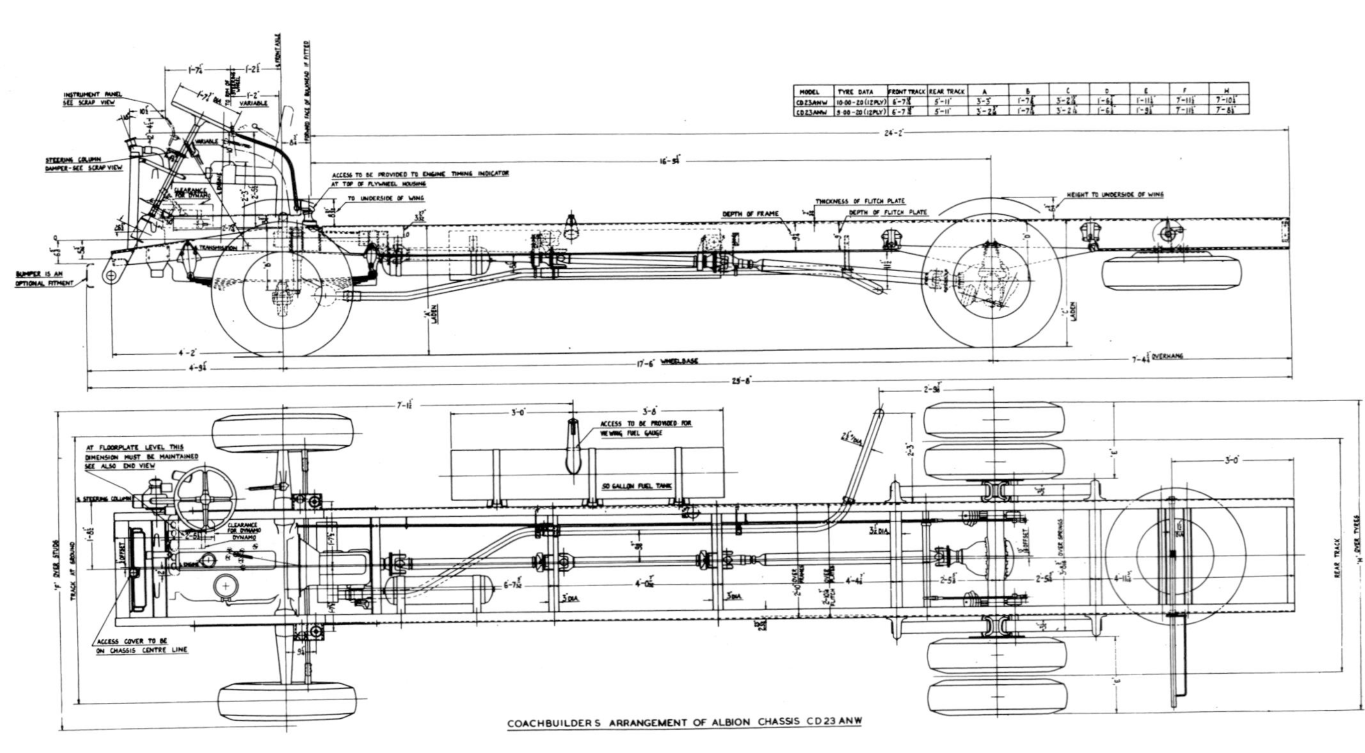

COACHBUILDERS ARRANGEMENT OF ALBION CHASSIS CD23 ANW

Before we leave behind the traditional looking Albions, let's take a glimpse at this final assortment.

The mixed Crowther fleet photographed in about 1960 includes Ford Thames Traders, ERFs, an elderly Foden and two Chieftains of 1955 and 1957. The BRS tipper is also a 1957 vehicle, whilst the date of the Reiver working in New South Wales is not certain. The spartan looking log hauler is one of two 130 bhp HD models that in 1959 had spent five arduous years extracting mahogany in Uganda. Their "cabs" were made of 3/8 in. mild steel plate. As testimony to the long lasting abilities of Albions, it is fitting to mention the 1950 Chieftain working for Miers Transport of Wolverhampton. It had covered 415,000 miles with one major overhaul by 1960 and was averaging 20.2 mpg.

Finally, there is a Scammell and Chieftain or Clydesdale behind a mysterious chassis. The chassis is designated CH.9XL which makes it a Chieftain, though it is to bear a Meteoor badge when it is bodied in Holland.

BRITISH ROAD SERVICES
STOWMARKET
3A374
ULD 538

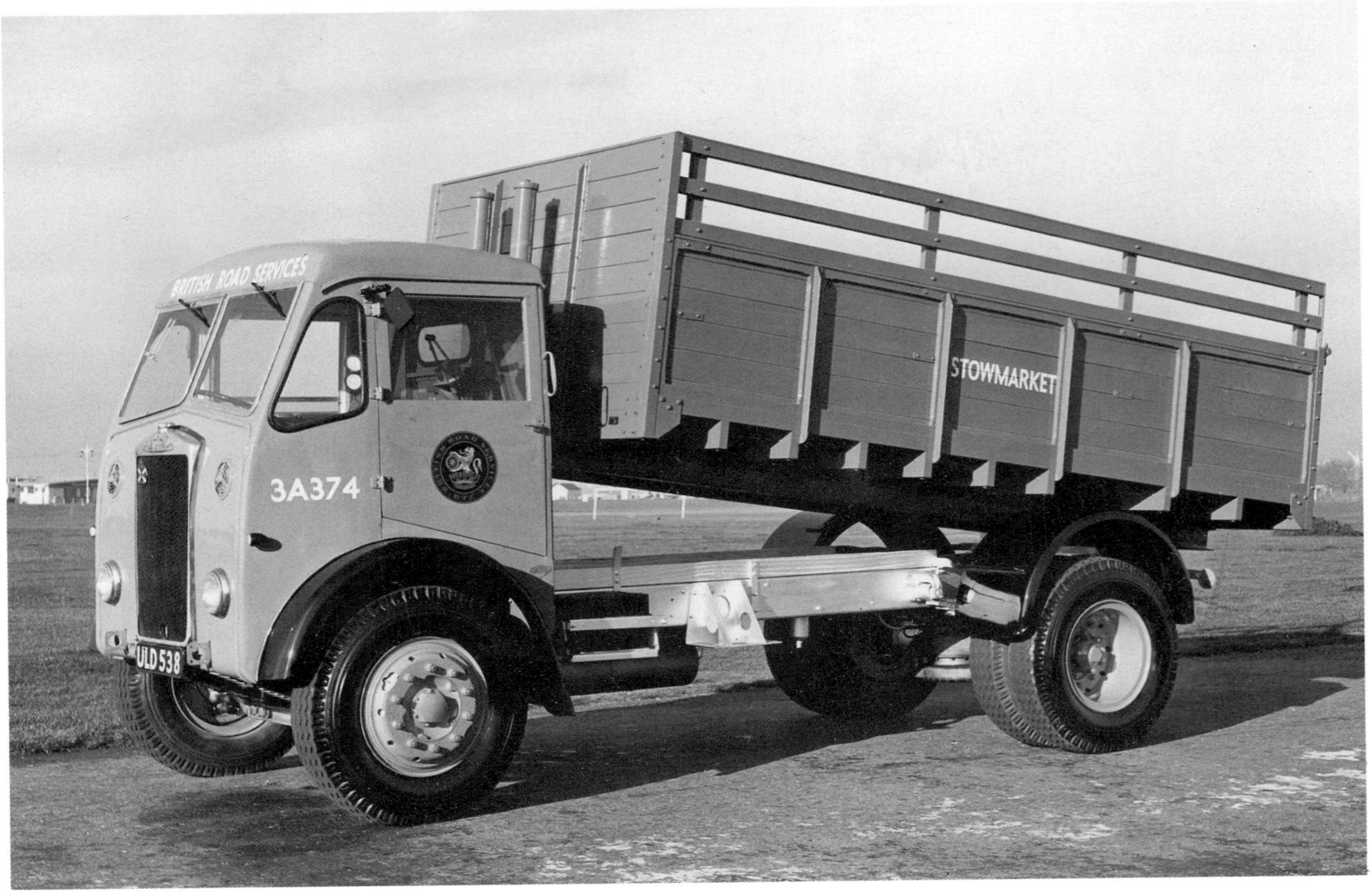

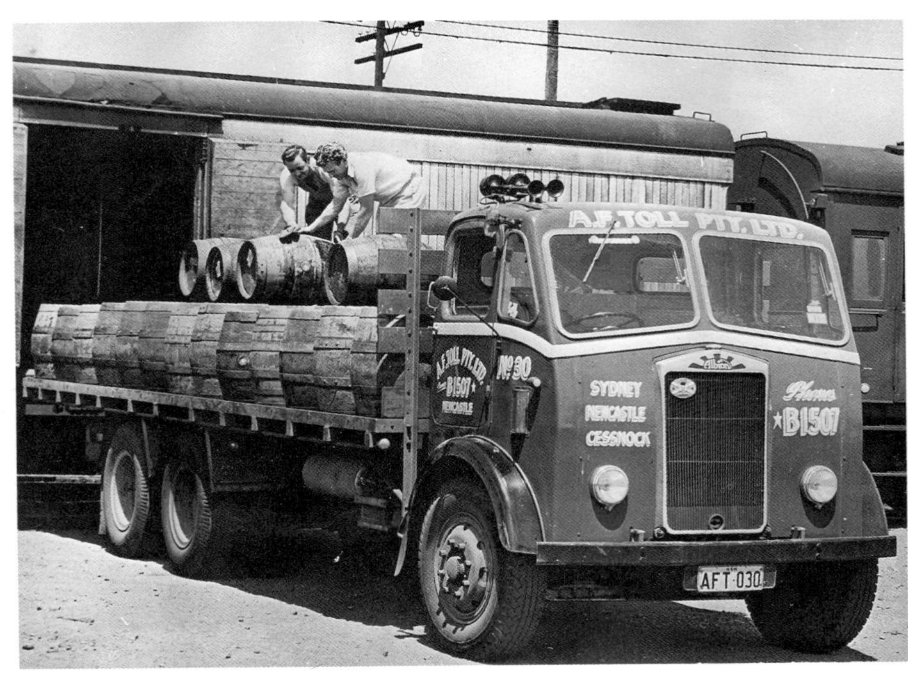

A.F. TOLL PTY. LTD.
No 30
SYDNEY
NEWCASTLE
CESSNOCK
Phone
B1507
AFT 030

TARKWA
ABOSSO URBAN COUNCIL

An interesting contrast between an export heavy duty cross-country bus for the Sudan in 1959 on a Reiver chassis, and two home-market Nimbus of the same period. The Reiver has 44 seat bodywork by MCW complete with tropical roof and overhead luggage bay, whilst the 31 seat Nimbus with Brewer's Motor Services has Willowbrook coachwork and is for one-man operation. The other Nimbus has unspecified 32 seat service bus coachwork.

A curious sideline in 1959 was the Albion Cuthbertson Biggar Buffalo, though the name soon changed to Water Buffalo. Biggar, incidentally, is a place in Scotland where J. A. Cuthbertson Ltd. had its factory and where today the Biggar Motor Museum holds many of the Albion archives that are not housed by the BMIHT at Studley. The Water Buffalo came in 14 and 24 ton sizes with 87 bhp Albion or 150 bhp Leyland engines and Self Changing Gears Pneumo-cyclic gearbox. R. A. Dyson built the 10 and 28 ton trailers for these unusual machines, one of which at any rate, was supplied for petroleum exploration in Nigeria. These four pictures show the 24 ton size with and without flotation equipment on test in Scotland.

Albion

A moment of great significance in the history of Albion was its adoption of the all steel LAD cab late in 1958. Both the new 9 ton Clydesdale with Leyland 0.375 six-cylinder diesel, and 7 ton Chieftain with Albion four-cylinder engine, featured a similar cab to the new Leyland Super Comet, though unlike it they had deep doors with the entrance step ahead of the wheel. Here an old alloy cab Albion picks up a load of new cabs from the makers, Motor Panels (Coventry) Ltd.

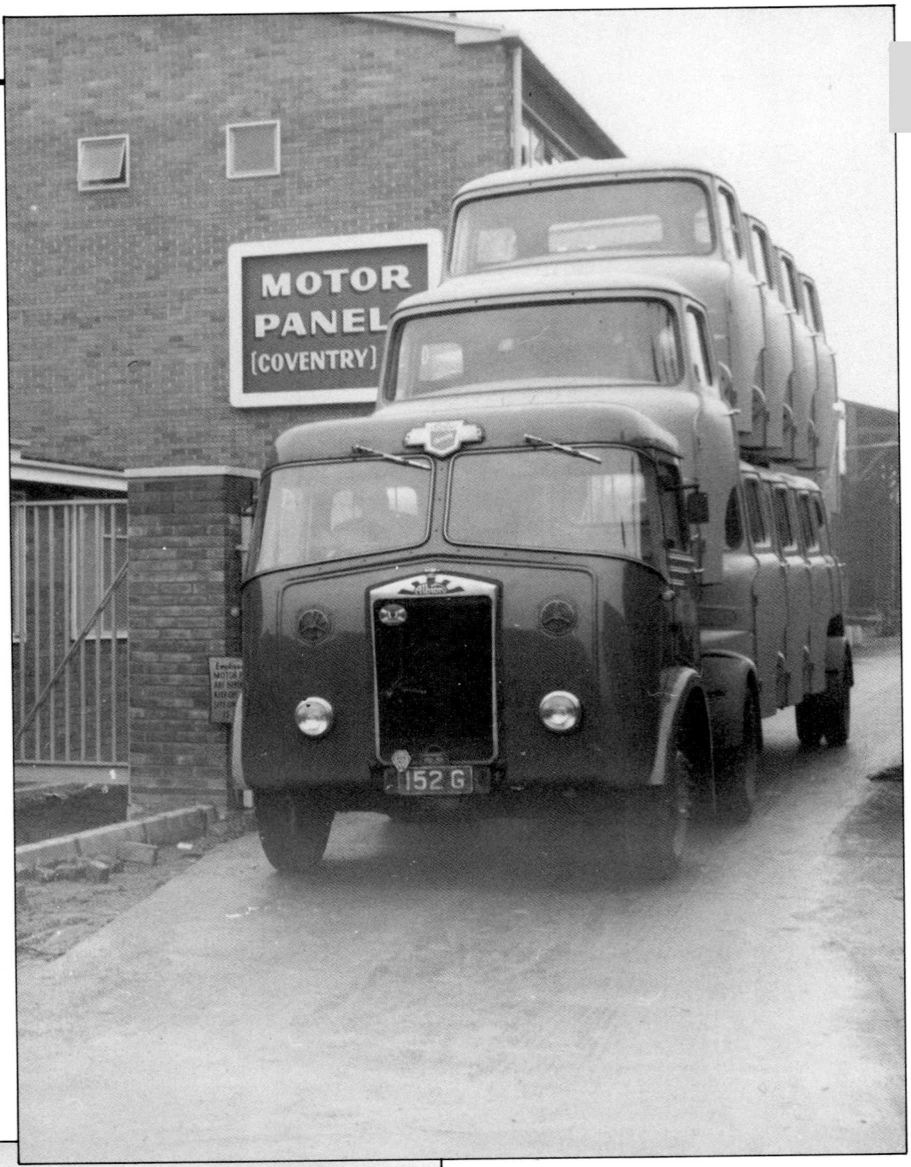

A strange combination on a 1959 Albion with the pressed metal front of the LAD but with more austere cab behind. LAD stood for Leyland, Albion and Dodge, the three factories which had shared the development and tooling costs at Motor Panels. All three contrived to make the standard cabs look different on their vehicles.

Some early views of the standard steel cab Albion range. The dropside has bodywork by Arlington, the 2,190 gallon fuel tanker is a CD21L Clydesdale, the Chieftain for Accra has a 1,000 gallon cesspool tank by Eagle, whilst the flat-bed grain lorry is one of the first Chieftains built, a CH3L of 1958.

HOWIE OF DUNLOP
R. HOWIE & SONS LTD.
PHONE 341 (4 LINES)
DUNLOP
HOWIE
MCS 690
UW - 3-16-3

ACCRA MUNICIPAL COUNCIL

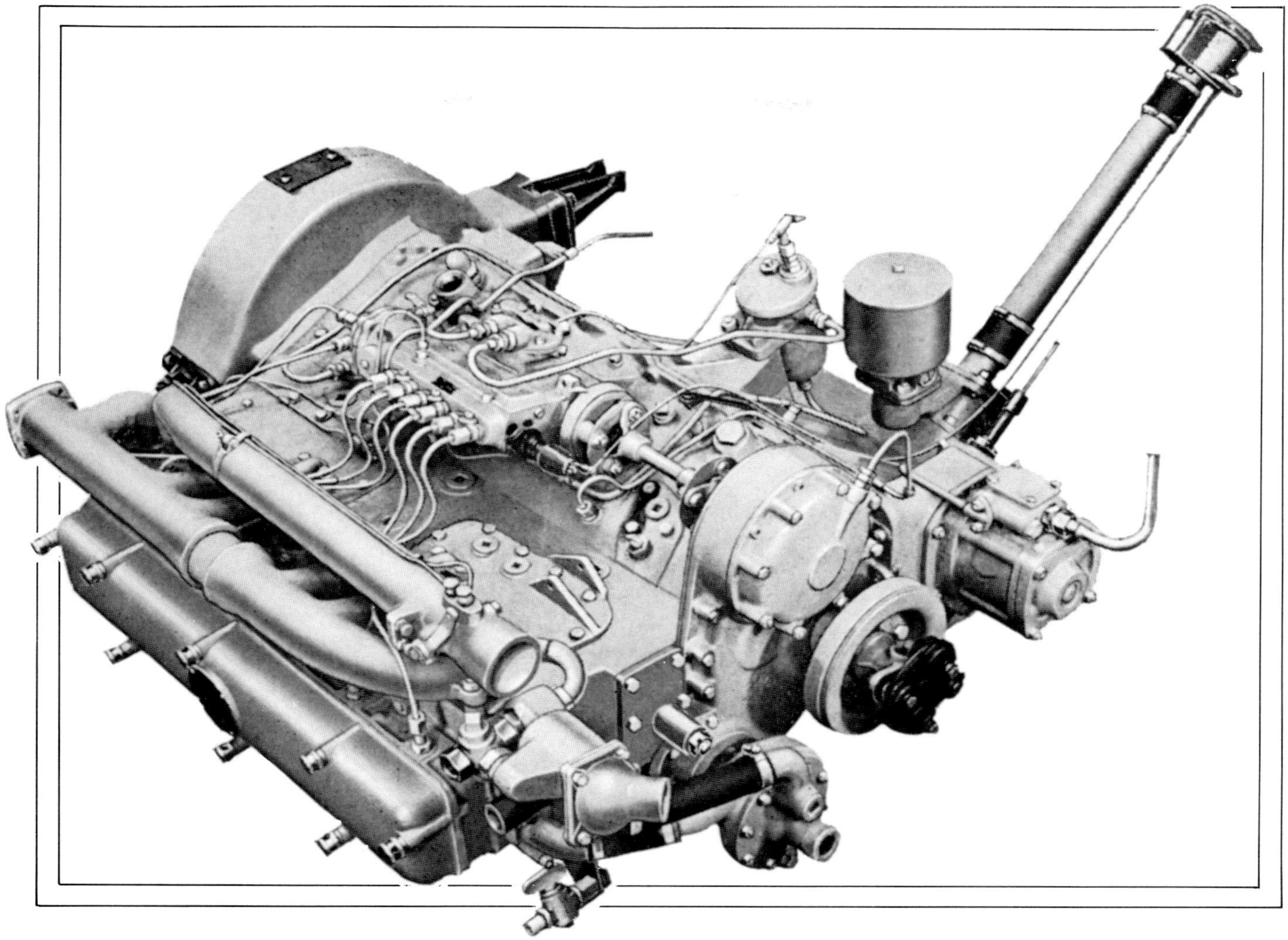

The Aberdonian of the 1958 to 1961 period was billed as an underfloor engined super-economy passenger chassis. It had a mid-mounted Leyland 0.350 engine with five-speed constant mesh gearbox. The brakes were of the vacuum hydraulic type and the chassis layout was similar to that of the smaller engined Nimbus and Claymore.

Shown here is a 1958 Plaxtons publicity photograph, the horizontal Leyland engine, and the front cover of a November 1959 sales brochure.

ABERDONIAN

UNDERFLOOR-ENGINED SUPER-ECONOMY PASSENGER CHASSIS

With 39 passenger luxury coachwork Unladen weight 5¼ tons

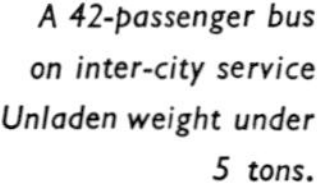

A 42-passenger bus on inter-city service Unladen weight under 5 tons.

A 30 ft. overall length, 8 ft. wide vehicle with gross laden weight of only 8½ tons

DESIGNED FOR HOME AND EXPORT MARKETS

L.680b

Albion

Nimbus

UNDERFLOOR ENGINED 31 SEATER LIGHTWEIGHT BUS CHASSIS WITH GROSS LADEN WEIGHT UNDER 6 TONS

Leaflet No. L. 688

THE ALBION 'Victor'

MODEL FT.39KA PASSENGER CHASSIS WITH OIL ENGINE

The Albion 'Victor' passenger chassis has been designed to meet the demand for a high-grade oil engined chassis of reasonably low weight, capable of a good performance in conjunction with outstanding economy of operation.

The chassis is of the straight framed type, suitable for full fronted bodywork. It is available in two wheelbases—16′ 0½″ and 16′ 11½″—providing ample space for bodies carrying up to 33 and 37 passengers respectively with an adequate bodyweight allowance.

The maximum gross vehicle weight of the 16′ 0½″ wheelbase chassis is 7-tons 14-cwt., and the 16′ 11½″ wheelbase chassis is suitable for a maximum gross vehicle weight of 8-tons.

In service in New Zealand — a 'Victor' 31 passenger bus

Among the many features to be noted are :-

- ★ Smooth running, efficient and economical 85 b.h.p. 4-cylinder diesel engine of advanced design.
- ★ 5-speed gearbox with constant mesh on all forward speeds with easy gear change.
- ★ Wide and long semi-elliptic road springs.
- ★ Hydraulic shock absorbers front and rear.
- ★ Vacuum assisted hydraulically operated brakes having effective liner area of 465 sq. ins.
- ★ Alternative frame with drop rear end for increased luggage capacity or low rear boarding platform.

A 'Victor' 32 passenger bus in service in the Gold Coast

Operating in Holland — a 'Victor' bus with left hand steering

The front cover of a 1958 sales brochure for the Nimbus (previous page), which was effectively the passenger version of the Claymore goods chassis with the same 4.1 litre 72 bhp four-cylinder diesel, which now incorporated many components from the Leyland 0.350 engine. The above catalogue page of similar vintage is for the export front engined Victor which had the 5.5 litre Albion EN.287 engine (introduced in 1960) and five-speed constant mesh gearbox (the Nimbus only had four ratios, but even so could regularly average 20 mpg).

The Reiver six-wheeler had first arrived in pre-LAD days but here is how it appeared with the new steel cab. The Talbot Transport example was new in 1961. To begin with the Reiver had choice of Albion four- or Leyland six-cylinder engines. From 1961 as the Super Reiver (still for 15½ tons gvw) it could have the Leyland Power Plus 0.400 6.54 litre 125 bhp diesel. The September 1960 coachbuilder's diagram is of a Super Reiver, as despite the Reiver heading, the more powerful Super model had an A after the model number. Note the non-reactive extra traction rear bogie introduced in 1960.

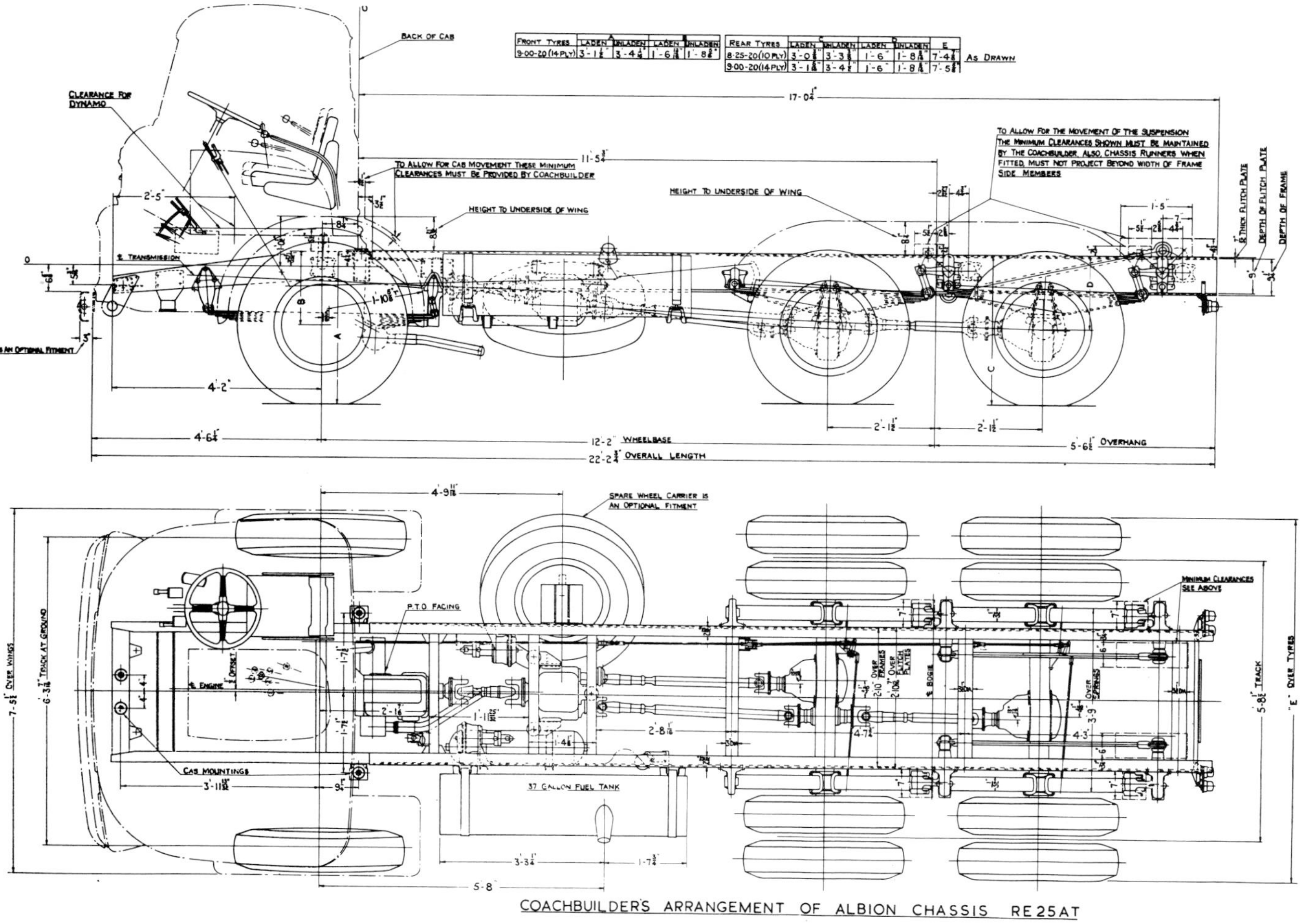

BACK OF CAB

CLEARANCE FOR DYNAMO

TO ALLOW FOR CAB MOVEMENT THESE MINIMUM CLEARANCES MUST BE PROVIDED BY COACHBUILDER

HEIGHT TO UNDERSIDE OF WING

TO ALLOW FOR THE MOVEMENT OF THE SUSPENSION THE MINIMUM CLEARANCES SHOWN MUST BE MAINTAINED BY THE COACHBUILDER. ALSO, CHASSIS RUNNERS WHEN FITTED, MUST NOT PROJECT BEYOND WIDTH OF FRAME SIDE MEMBERS

BUMPER IS AN OPTIONAL FITMENT

12-2" WHEELBASE

OVERALL LENGTH

OVERHANG

SPARE WHEEL CARRIER IS AN OPTIONAL FITMENT

P.T.O. FACING

CAB MOUNTINGS

37 GALLON FUEL TANK

MINIMUM CLEARANCES SEE ABOVE

COACHBUILDER'S ARRANGEMENT OF ALBION CHASSIS RE25AT

SCALE – ½" = 1 FOOT

New at the 1958 Commercial Motor Show was the Caledonian lightweight eight-wheeler with Leyland 0.600 engine and Leyland five-speed gearbox. It was only listed for three years and presumably accounted for few sales. Amongst the most unusual was this fuel tanker for National Benzole with Alfred Miles Ltd. cab and tank.

The remarkable economy of the Chieftain was particularly startling when compared with US gas guzzlers. As this 1960 advertisement shows, Yale Express System Inc. was suitably impressed. The Clydesdale was also offered in America but the usual difficulties facing a distant manufacturer with few back-up facilities discouraged more widespread use of Albions in America. It was to be several years before European truck producers were to make any serious inroads into such a difficult market. Meanwhile, Albion's traditional export territories were facing increasing competition from the Far East and Europe.

BREAK-THROUGH

Leylands drive in to the U.S. market - and add another chapter to the Leyland story

Selling refrigerators to Eskimos is child's play compared with selling British trucks to Americans on their home ground.

But Leylands have done it.

Today, Leyland Group vehicles—7-ton Albion Chieftains—are operating alongside 1,000 U.S.-built trucks in the fleet of Yale Express System Inc.—one of America's 'top-ten' hauliers. And orders for others are beginning to roll in.

What a wonderful proof of Leyland quality.

For make no mistake, what the Americans are sold on *is* quality . . . the quality which, in their own words "combines excellent workmanship with incredible economy." And here's the proof of that economy:

On stop-start general delivery work, involving between 32 and 40 pickups and drops per day for a five-day week, these Chieftains are returning fuel consumption figures of up to 21.6 miles per Imperial gallon.

Incredible? Well, perhaps so, by American standards. But to us who know Leylands—a commonplace. Just the natural outcome of that extra quality for which Leyland Group vehicles have been famed for years—*and* which is available to you.

ALBION MOTORS LTD.
SCOTSTOUN, GLASGOW.

LEYLAND MOTORS LTD.
LEYLAND, LANCS.

SCAMMELL LORRIES LTD.
WATFORD, HERTS.

SALES DIVISION: HANOVER HOUSE, HANOVER SQUARE, LONDON, W.1. TELEPHONE: MAYfair 8561

Advertisement published by Leyland Motors Ltd., during the month of June, 1960

In 1960 the Claymore received a five-, in place of four-speed constant mesh gearbox, as fitted to the Northern Dairies refrigerated van working in Northern Ireland. The 5 cu. yd. tipper is a CL35 model of 1959 for 165 cwt. gvw whilst the unusual looking platform truck with Leyland badge is a Claymore bodied in Holland.

The gradual adoption of the Leyland name, particularly in export markets, marked the beginning of the end for the Albion name on vehicles.

WILLIAM BIRTWISTLE ALLIED MILLS LTD
WILLIAM BIRTWISTLE ALLIED MILLS LTD
Cotton Spinners Manufacturers
PRESTON & BLACKBURN
720 HTF

An assortment of LAD cab Albions in a variety of roles. Most are fairly conventional, though the left-hand drive example with sleeper cab is rather more unusual. It took a consignment of Triumph Heralds to a show behind the Iron Curtain. The artics all have Scammell semi-trailers. The Hilton Gravel dumper is a Chieftain with Kays of Derby body and Edbro tipping gear.

HILTON
LTD.
HILTON
Nº DERBY.
HILTON GRAVEL

Hallamsteel
HALLAMSHIRE
HALLAM
24304
STEEL
Albion
766 EWE
The HALLAMSHIRE STEEL CO LTD SHEFFIELD

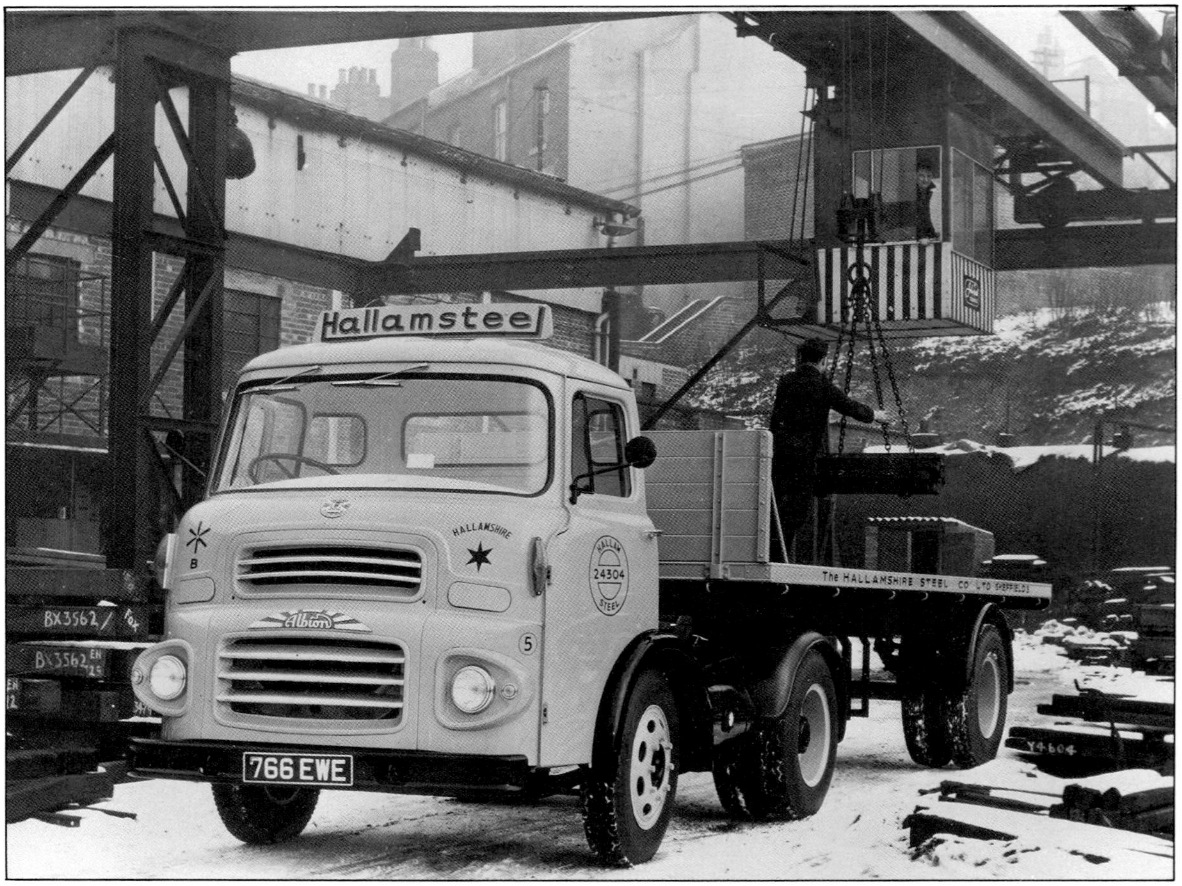

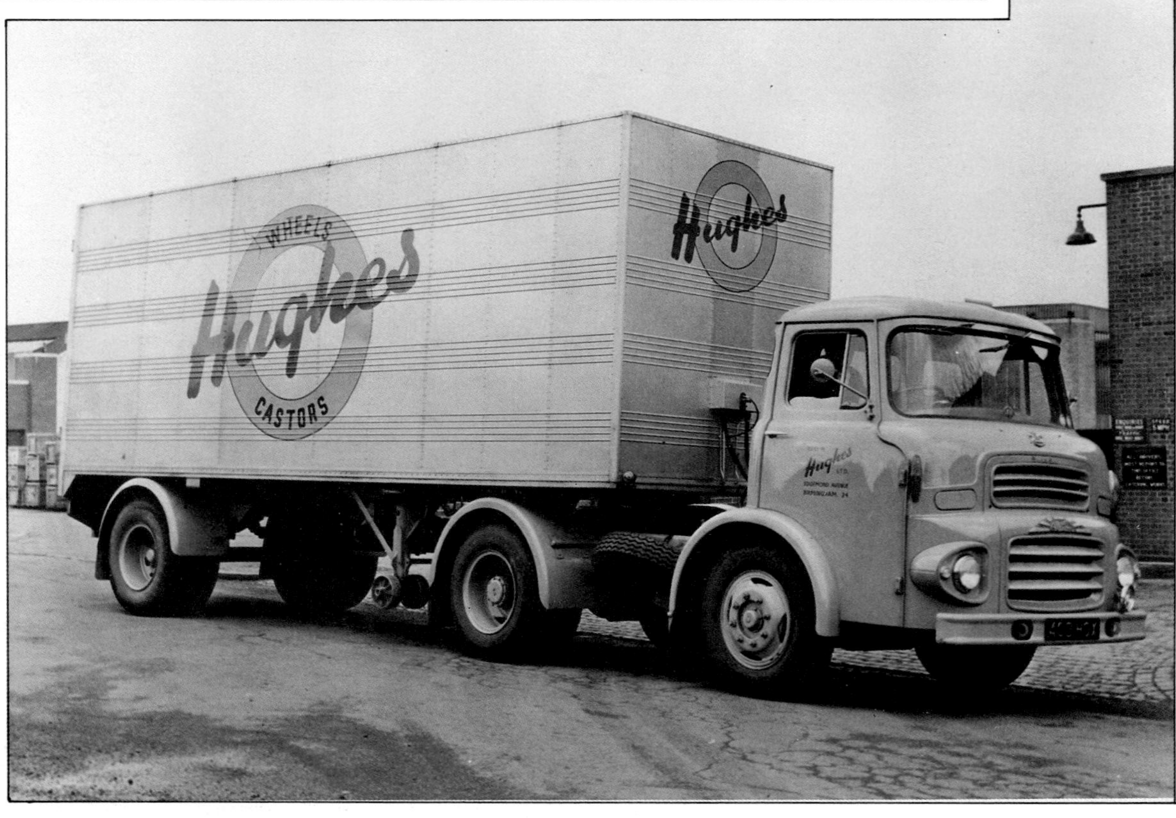

WHEELS
Hughes
CASTORS
Hughes

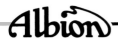

The Victor continued in its role as a tough, high clearance bus for rugged export markets. The 35 seat MCW bodied bus was destined for Kumasi whilst the VT17N was for Barbados with 35 seat Mulliner coachwork and LAD scuttle pressing. The FT series became the VT in 1959 and had the traditional four-cylinder Albion engine or the Leyland six-cylinder 0.350. It was also still possible to get the Clydesdale in passenger form and several with 55 seat single deck bodies were supplied to Rhodesia.

New in April 1962 was the Chieftain Super Six with Power-Plus EO.370 diesel developing 106 bhp and five- or six-speed Albion gearbox. Its four-cylinder Albion engined counterpart was now called Chieftain Series II. The latest in Ford Prefects is in the background, though the rest of the setting, with its stone setts and rails, is decidedly archaic and no doubt close to the Albion factory in Glasgow.

From 1961 a version of the Victor passenger chassis was offered specifically for low density loads of 4 tons – VT19AN model – to 5 tons – VT19AN(HD) model. Both had a wheelbase of 15'6" and had 94 bhp diesel with five- or six-speed gearboxes driving the famous Albion spiral bevel, hub reduction rear axle. The catalogue, of which the front cover is shown here, warned "that any attempt to employ them for the accomodation of loads of normal material can only result in gross overloading of the chassis, which is likely to lead to mechanical trouble!"

Albion VICTOR

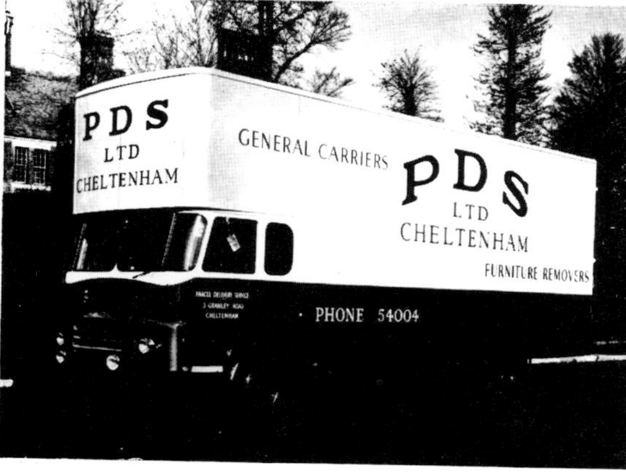

ENGINEERED AND DESIGNED BY ALBION MOTORS LIMITED

BUILT TO HANDLE BULKY LOADS!

Leaflet No. L.719B

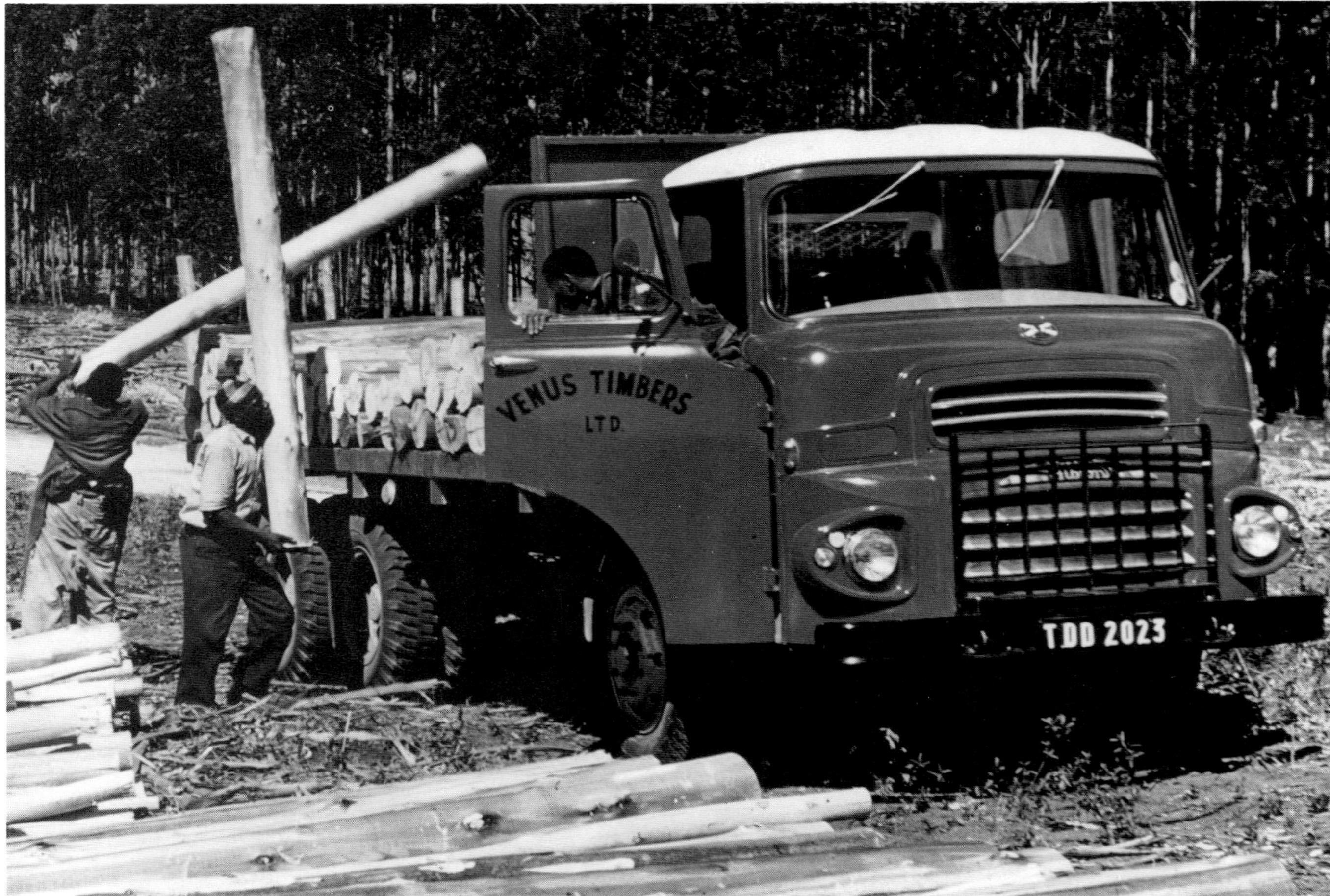

Africa continued to be a major market for Albion and here we have a Reiver working in the Eastern Transvaal in 1964. The hub reduction axles made half shaft breakages very unusual, even in harsh off-road work with semi-skilled drivers. Up in Tanganyika, the East African Railways and Harbours Administration had a fleet of 78 Victor buses and 134 lorries, all of which, apart from a few Leyland Hippos, were Albions and there were several other large fleets on the African continent. The curious little dumper for underground use was based on a Chieftain with torque converter transmission.

Some useful information from Albion's publicity department. The department also provided dealers with sheets showing standard printing blocks in various sizes that could be used in local press advertising or on letterheads.

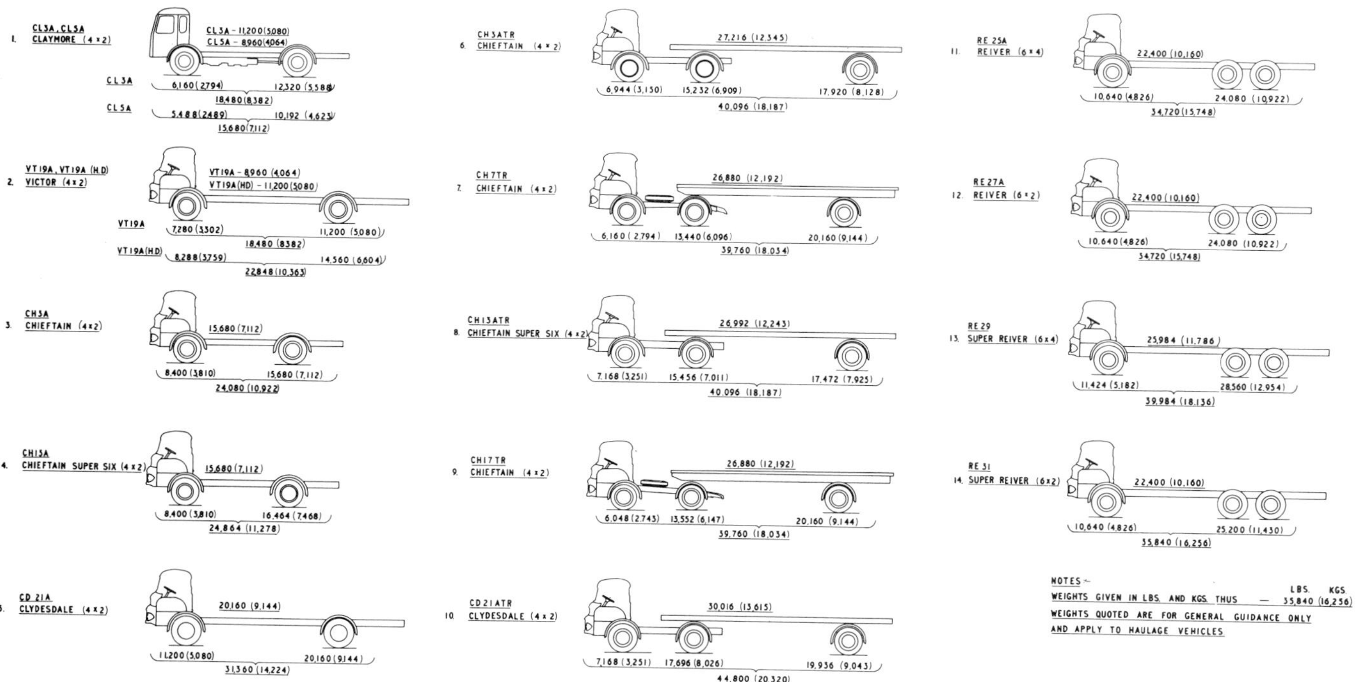

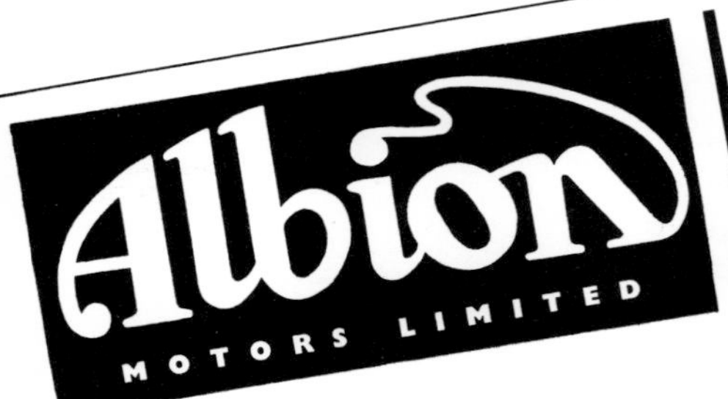

BLOCKS FOR PRESS ADVERTISING

Order by numbers from :—

"CLAYMORE"

PUBLICITY DEPT.
ALBION MOTORS LIMITED
SCOTSTOUN · GLASGOW W.4

CL 53

CL 52

CL 51

CL 56

CL 55

CL 54

CL 57

CL 58

CL 59

CL 62

CL 61

CL 60

BLOCKS FOR PRESS ADVERTISING

Order by numbers from :—

"REIVER"

PUBLICITY DEPT.
ALBION MOTORS LIMITED
SCOTSTOUN · GLASGOW W.4

RE 201

RE 202

RE 203

RE 204

RE 205

RE 206

RE 207

RE 208

RE 209

RE 210

RE 211

RE 212

Rather surprisingly Albion returned to the double decker market in 1961 with the Lowlander. It had the Leyland 0.600 diesel with Pneumo-cyclic or synchromesh gearbox and the offset driveline and stepped axle shown here. Gross vehicle weight was 13 tons $4^1/2$ cwt. and overall height was under 13'6".

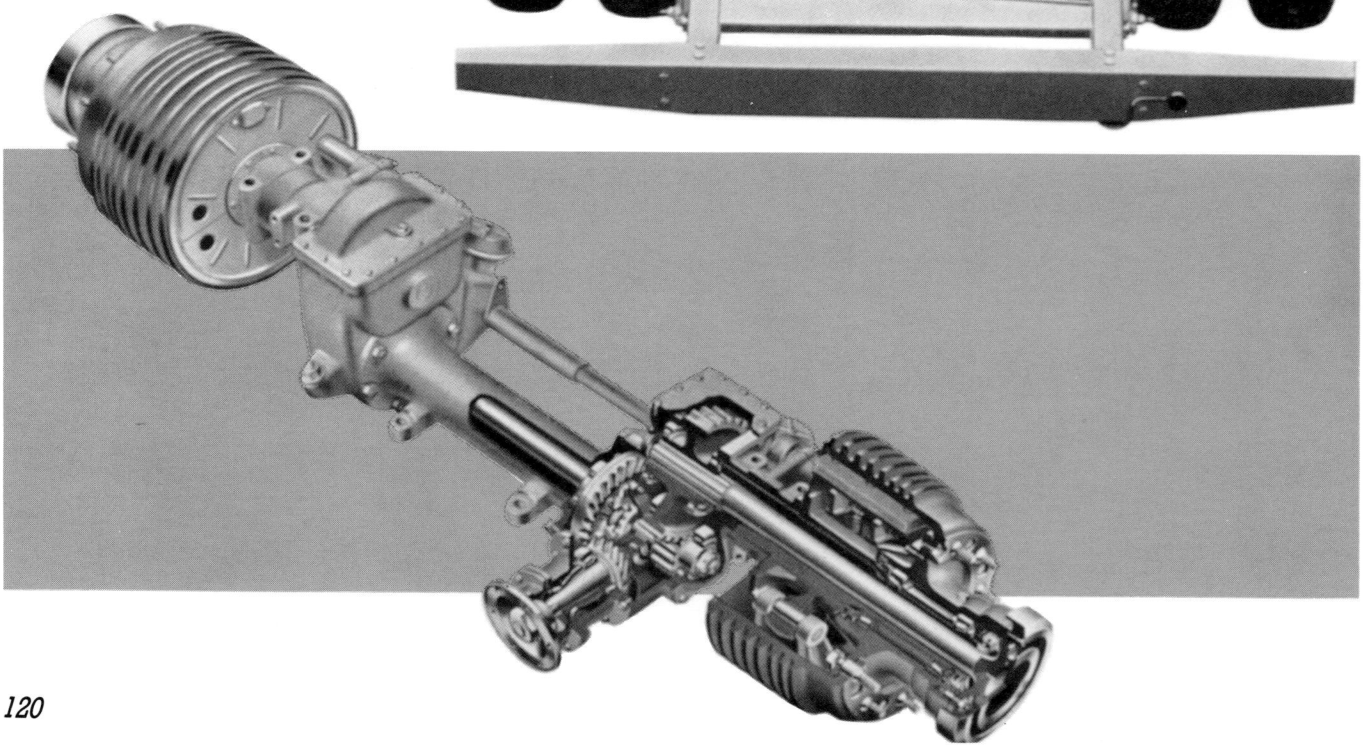

In 1963 Carmichael and Sons (Worcester) Ltd. used the Chieftain chassis as the basis for their Firechief appliance. It had a 125 bhp Leyland 0.400 diesel with six-speed gearbox. It had a fibreglass front and composite steel or alloy bodywork. Tank capacity of up to 1,000 gallons could be specified with Gwynne 600, 750 or 1,000 gpm pumps.

From late in 1964 several Albion models gained the excellent Sankey-built Group Ergomatic tilt cab. In the Albion application it was said to have lighter panels, which is quite possible because for heavy duty work the old LAD cab continued to be specified. Shown here is a Super Clydesdale on test with weights and trade plates, a Super Reiver 20 (model RE33L) with sheeted load and the same type in chassis cab form and a bodybuilder's layout plan for a Super Clydesdale tractive unit.

ALBION

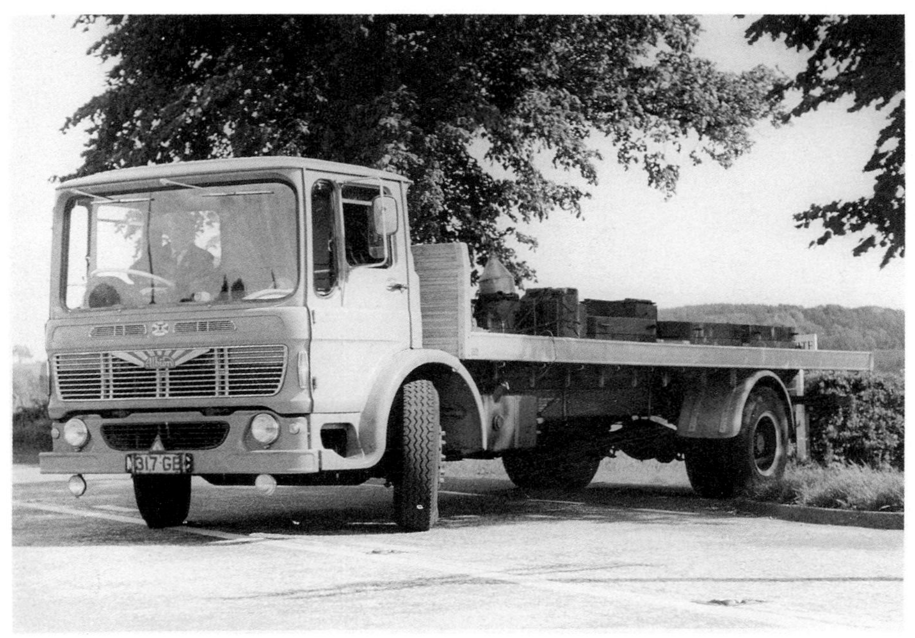

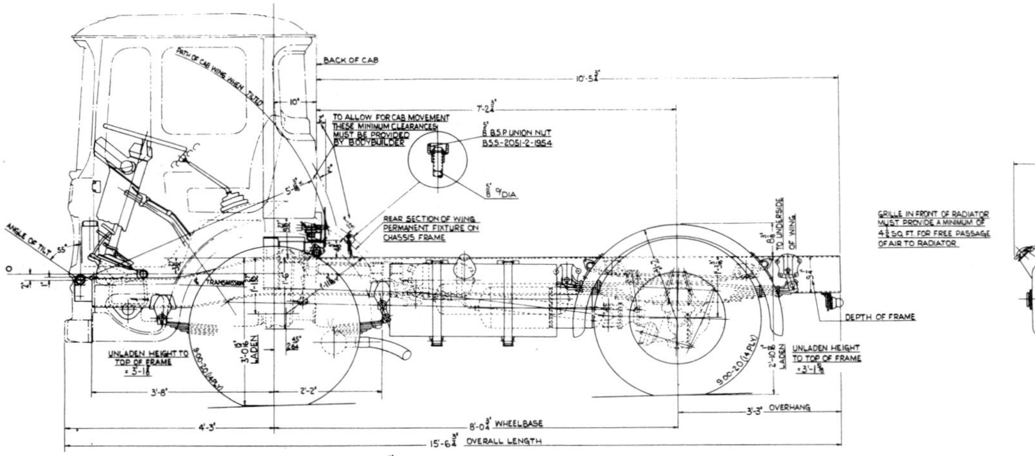

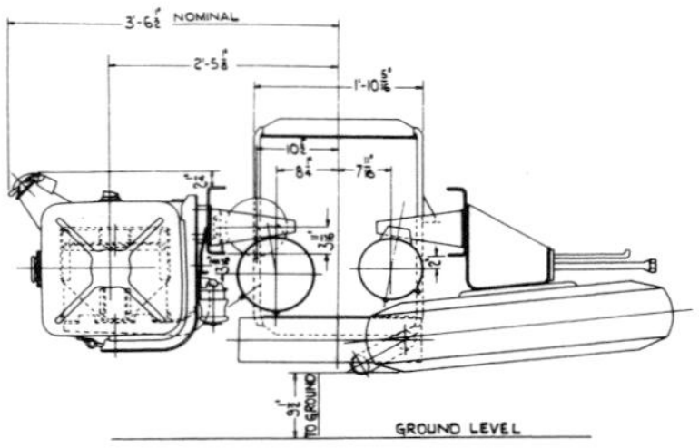

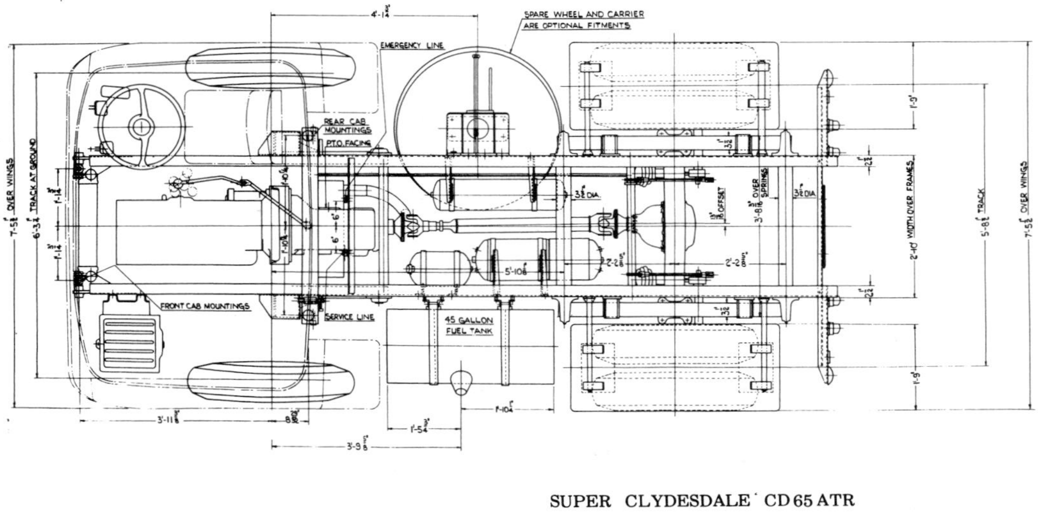

BACK OF CAB
10'-5¾"
7'-2¾"
TO ALLOW FOR CAB MOVEMENT THESE MINIMUM CLEARANCES MUST BE PROVIDED BY BODYBUILDER
B.S.P. UNION NUT BS5-2051-2-1954
ANGLE OF TILT 55°
REAR SECTION OF WING PERMANENT FIXTURE ON CHASSIS FRAME
TO UNDERSIDE OF WING
DEPTH OF FRAME
UNLADEN HEIGHT TO TOP OF FRAME
LADEN
3'-8"
2'-2"
4'-3"
8'-0¼" WHEELBASE
3'-3" OVERHANG
15'-6¾" OVERALL LENGTH

3'-6¼" NOMINAL
2'-5⅛"
GRILLE IN FRONT OF RADIATOR MUST PROVIDE A MINIMUM OF 4½ SQ. FT. FOR FREE PASSAGE OF AIR TO RADIATOR
GROUND LEVEL

4'-1¾"
SPARE WHEEL AND CARRIER ARE OPTIONAL FITMENTS
EMERGENCY LINE
REAR CAB MOUNTINGS
P.T.O. FACING
FRONT CAB MOUNTINGS
SERVICE LINE
45 GALLON FUEL TANK
7'-5⅛" OVER WINGS
6'-3⅞" TRACK AT GROUND
3'-8⅛" OVER SPRINGS
2'-10" WIDTH OVER FRAMES
5'-8⅛" TRACK
7'-5⅛" OVER WINGS
3'-11⅛"
1'-5¾"
1'-10⅛"
3'-9⅛"

NOTES:-

1. CAB INCLUDING FRONT WINGS SUPPLIED AND FITTED BY A.M. LTD.
2. REAR WINGS SUPPLIED AND FITTED BY A.M. LTD.
3. RUBBER AND LEATHER PARTS NOT TO BE PAINTED
4. LAMPS TO CONFORM TO M.O.T. REGULATIONS
5. IMPORTANT:- COACHBUILDER MUST NOT DRILL HOLES FOR ANY PURPOSE WHATSOEVER IN TOP OR BOTTOM FLANGES OF FRAME
6. WELDING ON CHASSIS FRAME IS PROHIBITED
7. TURNTABLE TO BE LOCATED ON CHASSIS SO THAT KING-PIN IS A MAXINUM OF 12" FORWARD OF REAR AXLE

SUPER CLYDESDALE' CD 65 ATR

New Construction and Use Regulations led Albion to develop a new rear engined Viking in collaboration with the Scottish Bus Group, for one-man operation. It was ready in 1965 and took advantage of the fact that rear overhang was allowed to be sixty per cent of the wheelbase length. Seating for 40/45 passengers was provided. The Viking had a Leyland 0.400 125 bhp diesel (or 0.370 106 bhp for some export models) and 5/6-speed gearbox.

The complete bus shown overleaf has Walter Alexander bodywork made in Falkirk.

GLASGOW 8B
Midland
HWG 524E

A couple of Albions in unusual places. The Super Reiver RE29N with 0.400 diesel was for communist East Germany and had a Duramin bulk grain tipping body. The Clydesdale belonged to Elie Marclay of Monthey in the Swiss Canton of Valais. It collected softwood in the mountains for conversion to chipboard and paper.

Particularly for export Scammell developed a 4 x 4 version of the Chieftain Super Six in 1967. It was known as the Chieftain 71 and had a Leyland 0.370 engine with two-range five-speed gearbox. The front drive axle was converted from a hub reduction rear axle with the addition of flash butt welded flanges to which were bolted cast steel swivels. In best Albion tradition, the chassis was of bolted construction. Here we have a chassis on test and a location filming unit for Wolper Productions of Hollywood with bodywork by Sparshatt, that included generator, refrigerator, Hipope tailboard lift, Martin Harper winch and Whitlock crane-cum-aerial seat.

Albion
262 GB

Hidden under that unusually styled fibreglass cab complete with pictures of a highland soldier in action on the front panels was a Chieftain Super Six. Lambert Engineering (Glasgow) Ltd. of Coatbridge had to fit a larger cab to permit the driver to face rearwards when operating their Hydrocon Highlander six ton crane, of which considerable numbers were built, some on Leyland Comet chassis.

Through the 1960s Albion's increasing speciality became transmission components for the expanding Leyland Group. In 1960 the adjoining cab and bodywork factory of Robert Rogerson & Co Ltd was demolished to make way for a new Gear Shop. In 1968 BMC, or to be more accurate, British Motor Holdings, because it also controlled the Jaguar, Daimler and Guy empire by then, merged with Leyland. The old Austin and Morris-Commercial ranges had been moved to production facilities in Scotland at Bathgate and in 1970 these became known as Leyland Redlines, production finally ending in 1984/5.

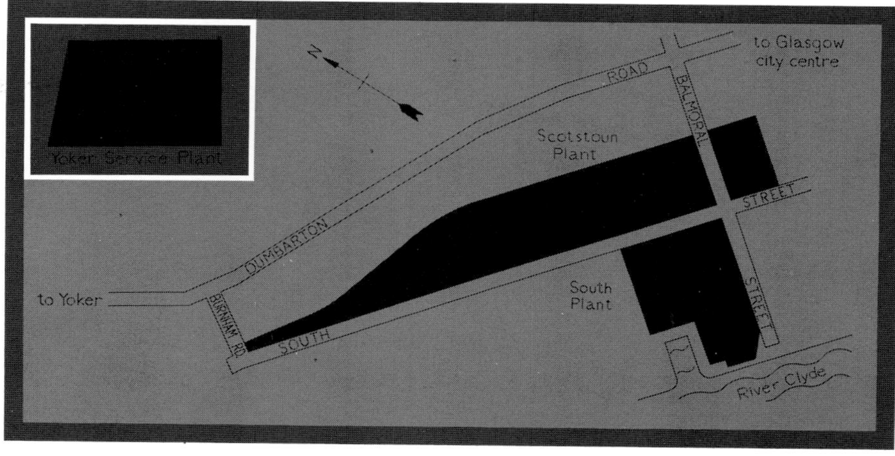

The Albion plant had meanwhile been given a £2 million modernisation in 1966 and the adjoining South Works for axle production acquired from Harland & Wolff in 1969. At that stage the Albion workforce totalled 3,500 and the factory floorspace covered 1½ million square feet (116.129 m²). The 750 ft. (229 m) moving chassis production line could handle various vehicle sizes from 9 to 24 tons gvw and with the end of Albion chassis production it was dismantled and re-instated at the Watford Plant of Scammell. Over at Yoker three hundred vehicles could be repaired and serviced per month and the former Halley factory also was responsible for Final Inspection and CKD packing for export.

Shown are various views in the factories, a hub reduction axle of the type made famous from 1958 and a ten-speed Synchro-Splitter gearbox.

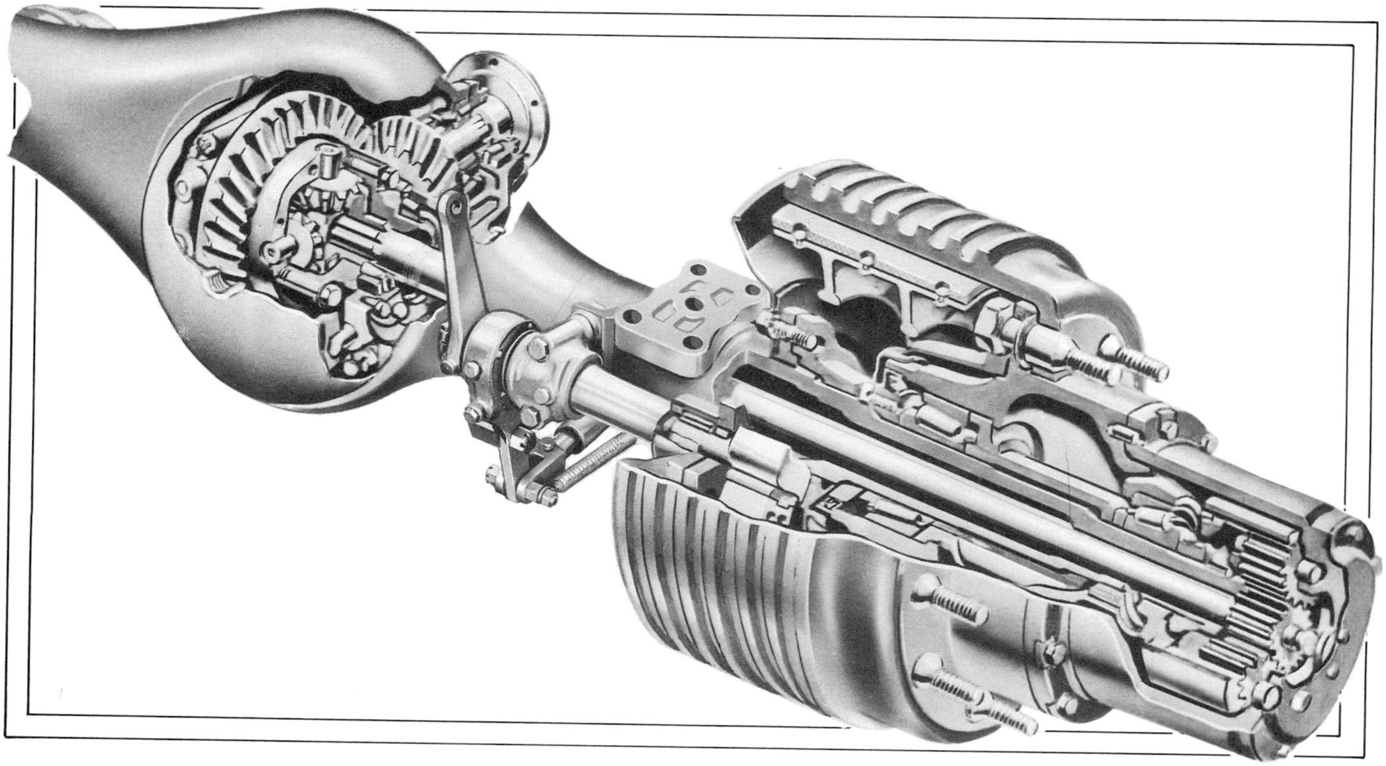

ALBION
MOTORS LTD
GLASGOW
SCOTLAND
MADE IN
SCOTLAND
Albion
AUSTRALIA

Glasgow continued to place the occasional bus order with Albion. The only problem was that Scotstoun only produced rugged, high clearance export single deckers by then. To get round this difficulty Leyland Atlanteans, like this 1967/8 example, were badged as Albions. The photograph dates from 1975, when Glasgow was celebrating the eight-hundredth anniversary of its Burgh Charter.

A Clydesdale at work in 1969 in the sort of tough environment that had become the marque's forte. Albion four-wheelers were regularly found as semi-off-road tippers, whilst the six-wheelers were becoming the backbone of the ready-mix concrete industry. Note the attractive gold leaf lettering and lining – a familiar feature on trucks working in Scotland to this day.

The aerial Albion is a Clydesdale being hoisted in Johannesburg to help in the construction of the Standard Bank building.

With the acquisition of AEC back in 1962, Leyland had yet another source of components at its disposal. In 1968 Albion needed a more powerful engine for its largest truck mixer chassis, the Reiver 129, and it chose the AV505 8.2 litre AEC diesel with AEC ten-speed range change gearbox. Output was 151 bhp, which gave the 44,800 lbs. (20,321 kg) gvw vehicle an impressive performance. Note the radius arms above the rear of the chassis for Albion's non-reactive high mobility rear suspension.

Earlier we showed a chassis destined for Holland as a Meteoor. Here we have a complete Meteoor at the Amsterdam Show in 1966. It had a cab by Jaro of Steenbergen in place of the more expensive Ergomatic tilt type (as seen on the Leyland in the background), or the cramped and, dare one say ugly, fixed Vista Vue LAD type.

BUYING A BUS

FOR SEMI-COACH WORK OR SUBURBAN OPERATION

Built on to Albion, Leyland, B.M.C., Bedford, Ford or Hino chassis with full range of seating types. Body features to suit your individual requirements from our Body Check List.

SUBURBAN REAR ENGINED ALBION VIKING

BRISBANE Nº16

REDLANDS BUS SERVICE PTY LTD

ALBION

Albion buses continued to be exported all over the world. This rear engined Viking appeared in a 1971 advertisement for the bodybuilder MBS of Brisbane, NSW. The front engined Viking also had quite a following in Australia, where a new version in the early 1970s had separate air braking systems on the front and rear axles. Power came from the Leyland 401 developing 150 bhp.

The rear view is of an attractive Park Royal bodied 41 seat coach tested by John Moon for the *Leyland Journal* in 1967.

ALBION
CLYDESDALE

Some late examples of Ergomatic cabbed Albions are featured here. The milk tanker version has 2,100 gallon bodywork by Associated Metal Works of Glasgow. The tipper chassis with straight frame for extra strength is a Reiver RE40 which was new in 1970 and was for 22 ton gvw. It and the Clydesdale 24 tons GTW artic introduced in 1969 at the Scottish Motor Show, had the turbocharged version of the Leyland 401 engine developing 155 bhp and revised frontal styling reminiscent of Leylands with the Fixed Head 500 engine. The new cab was to be the last shown by Albion at the London Motor Show. At their traditional showcase at the Glasgow Show there was nothing new for Albion, though there was a Scottish newcomer in the shape of the shortlived Argyle Christina 16 tonner.

TENNANT FORTH
Look well on Milk
TENNANT
FORTH
Albion
BVD 243J

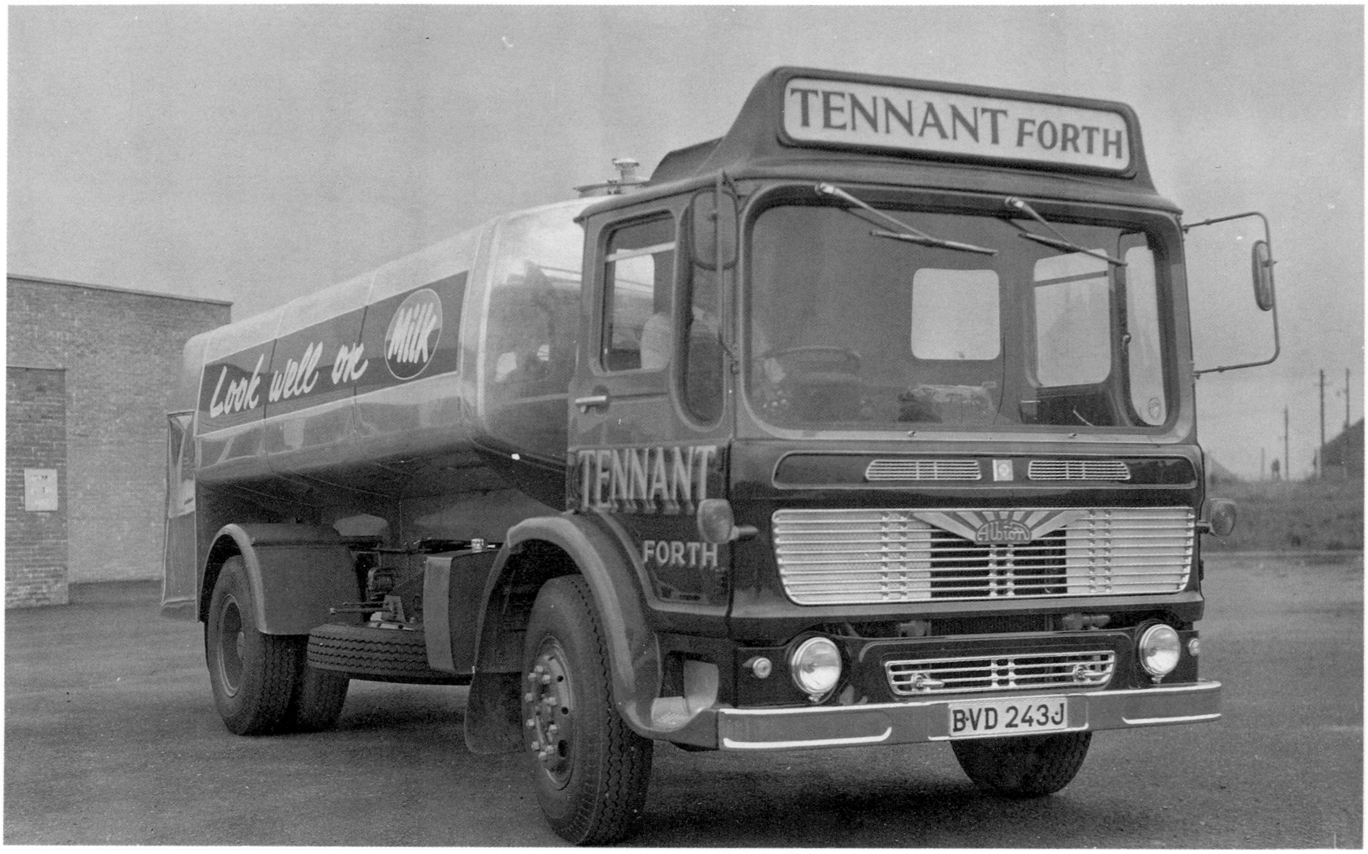

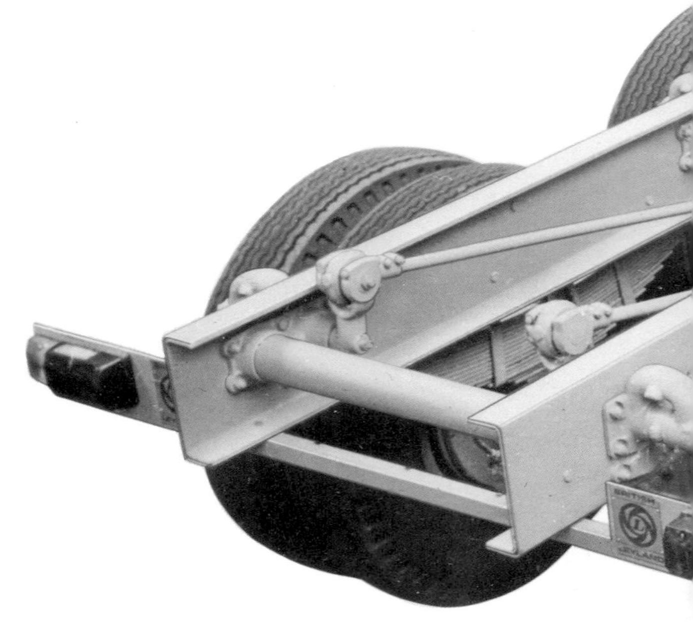

Though the Aberdonian had not lasted long in Britain, there was one final Albion rigid eight for Australia known as the Cameronian. Here we see one in 1969 with Dumpmaster rubbish equipment belonging to Industrial Waste Collection (Vic) Pty Ltd. The Cameronian was developed specially by the Leyland Motor Corporation of Australia.

In 1972 a major shake-up in the Leyland Group saw Albion changing its name to Leyland (Glasgow) and continuing to make the Chieftain 13.5 ton rigid, the Clydesdale 16 ton rigid and 24 ton tractor unit and the Reiver 24 ton tipper as well as export bus chassis and components for the rest of the group. The new range announced 1st September utilised the 400 engine and the same G-type cab as used by the Bathgate Redline Leylands that had been inherited from the old BMC FJ series. The new range was rightly popular, particularly the Reiver, which was Britain's biggest selling 24 tonner, and output by the 2830 personnel at the Albion plants was running at 170 vehicles per week in 1978, plus 308 gearboxes and 300 axles. The G cab was updated in 1980, when its outward appearance changed with the substitution of flush Leyland lettering, and at that stage Albion ceased to assemble vehicles. In 1981 the all-new Leyland Constructor and Freighter replaced the last of the Albion-origin goods models. (See *The Illustrated History of Leyland Trucks* in this series).

Between 1980 and 1982 the axle facilities of Leyland, Guy and Alford & Alder were moved to Albion, followed by the lighter axles from Bathgate. At that stage the Yoker factory was closed down.

THOMAS. R. TUCK LTD.
HAULAGE CONTRACTORS
PHONE
ALDRIDGE
52597
LEYLAND
SRE 659L
LEYLAND
CHIEFTAIN
BRITISH
LEYLAND

In February 1970 a new bus and coach marketing organisation within British Leyland took over the sales and servicing of vehicles by Leyland, AEC, Albion, Bristol, Daimler, Guy and Leyland National. The ranges were rationalised and after this Albion continued to make its Clydesdale and front engined Viking, both with hub reduction axles, 400 engines and manual gearboxes. Here we see an example of the larger model heavily laden in Africa in the late 1970s.

A preserved Albion comes to the rescue of an oldtimer that will be restored for posterity.

Though there were no more vehicles marketed under the Albion name, the factory continued to be busy in the Leyland organisation, and in Leyland DAF following the merger of 1987. 1,100 men were employed in the mid 1980s making 30,000 axles per year and £9 million was spent on modernising the adjoining former GKN factory, which is now Albion's headquarters. Following the closure of the North Works at the end of 1987, output is to be increased to 50,000 axles of 6.5 to 65 tonnes capacity per year, using 41 per cent less floor space, 57 per cent less individual tooling and 30 per cent lower fixed costs for a 30 per cent increase in productivity. It is perhaps significant that DAF chose not to continue with the Leyland engine plant nor Scammell factory, but has supported the modernisation of the Albion facility, which now has robot welders and many new machine tools. Meanwhile, trucks and buses bearing Albion's familiar Scottish model names continue to earn their keep around the world, and there are still many true Albions at work, despite the fact that the youngest of them is now almost twenty years old. With almost a thousand employees Albion is still the largest single motor industry operation in Scotland – long may it continue.